JOHN BETJEMAN'S
COLLECTED POEMS
ENLARGED EDITION

JOHN BETJEMAN'S COLLECTED POEMS

Enlarged Edition

COMPILED
AND WITH AN INTRODUCTION BY
The Earl of Birkenhead

LONDON
JOHN MURRAY

© John Betjeman 1958, 1959, 1960, 1961, 1962,
1963, 1964, 1965, 1966

*First published 1958
Eighth impression 1960
Second edition (with additional poems) 1962
Fifth impression 1968
Third edition (with addition of all poems
published in* High and Low) *1970*

Fifth Impression 1976

*Printed in Great Britain by
Butler & Tanner Ltd, Frome and London*

0 7195 2698 1

Contents

vi

* Not published separately in book form.

† Previously published in book form and added to the second edition of *Collected Poems*.

Acknowledgements

Grateful acknowledgement is made to the Editors of *Punch, The London Magazine, The New Yorker, Harper's Bazaar, The Saturday Book, The Cornhill, The Atlantic Monthly, Encounter, The Observer, Vogue, Weekend Telegraph* and *The Philbeach Quarterly*. " The Harvest Hymn " was published as a letter in *The Farmers Weekly*.

The author is grateful to his friends John Hanbury Angus Sparrow, Lord Birkenhead and Thomas Edward Neil Driberg. The first made and introduced the original selection for *Selected Poems;* the second advised on the first edition of *Collected Poems* and the third corrected grammar and punctuation, and changed some lines for the better.

Introduction to First Edition

Many years ago, when I was an undergraduate at
Oxford, Sir Maurice Bowra remarked to me of John
Betjeman, who was then writing such verses as
" The 'Varsity Students' Rag " and other juvenilia :
" Betjeman has a mind of extraordinary originality ;
there is no one else remotely like him." He has
remained so until the present time, and is now a
lonely and arresting figure in modern poetry.
Among the many ways in which he differs from most
of his fellow-poets is that his poems are commercially
successful to his publishers and himself.

Mr. John Sparrow, writing a preface to an earlier
volume of Betjeman's poems, truly observed after
quoting from the brilliant piece " Sunday in Ire-
land ": " Plainly what inspired the writer of those
stanzas was a sense of place." Elsewhere he said :
" In other words he is not a Nature poet, like
Wordsworth, but a landscape poet like Crabbe and,
like Crabbe, he is the painter of the particular, the
recognizable landscape ; his trees are not merely
real trees with their roots in the earth, they are
conifers with their roots in the red sand of Camberley,
feathery ash in leathery Lambourne, or forsythia in
the Banbury Road."

This sense of place, so varied and so tender, has
led Betjeman into a calculated risk, that of being
typed as the poet of the suburbs, and many have
wrongly assumed this addiction to be either a pose

or a hoax on the public, and yet another example of that double-bluff humour in which his somewhat perverse mind undoubtedly delights. That is, however, a false impression, for his searching visual powers, as I shall try to show, are by no means confined to the suburban scene. It is true that he loves it, and has a deeply sympathetic insight into the minds of those who dwell there. He likes the throng at the Home and Colonial, and what they talk about; he likes the speckled laurels in suburban gardens, the brilliant arcade and the electric train and Charing Cross Station hunched over the river in the sunset.

His poetic mind is not, however, concentrated on such scenes to the exclusion of everything else. He has the true poet's instinct of registering impressions wherever he finds himself. This power not only to absorb but to set down in words is probably what separates the ordinary man from the poet and resides in the fact that the latter is articulate. Many have loved the Essex countryside but few could thus express that love:

> And as I turn the colour-plates
>   Edwardian Essex opens wide,
> Mirrored in ponds and seen through gates,
>   Sweet uneventful countryside.
>
> Like streams the little by-roads run
>   Through oats and barley round a hill
> To where blue willows catch the sun
>   By some white weather-boarded mill. . . .

It is above all Cornwall, where he spent much of his youth and to which he annually returns, that most deeply stirs this poet's senses—the villages with their winding streets and swarthy children on the doorsteps, the derelict tin mines, the daffodil fields, the nodding fuchsias, and above all the sea. Betjeman writes splendidly and with a strong flavour of the past about the forbidding coast where the galleons splintered on the rocks and the bones of Spanish sailors were strewn. It excites him most in storm, and in " Trebetherick " he recalls yearningly the vanished joys of childhood:

We used to picnic where the thrift
  Grew deep and tufted to the edge;
We saw the yellow foam-flakes drift
  In trembling sponges on the ledge
Below us, till the wind would lift
  Them up the cliff and o'er the hedge.
      Sand in the sandwiches, wasps in the tea,
      Sun on our bathing-dresses heavy with the
        wet,
      Squelch of the bladder-wrack waiting for the
        sea,
      Fleas round the tamarisk, an early cigarette.

              .   .   .   .

      Waves full of treasure then were roaring up
        the beach,
      Ropes round our mackintoshes, waders warm
        and dry,
      We waited for the wreckage to come swirling
        into reach,
      Ralph, Vasey, Alastair, Biddy, John and I.

Then roller into roller curled
  And thundered down the rocky bay,
And we were in a water-world
  Of rain and blizzard, sea and spray,

And one against the other hurled
  We struggled round to Greenaway.
        Blesséd be St. Enodoc, blesséd be the wave,
        Blesséd be the springy turf, we pray, pray to
          thee,
        Ask for our children all the happy days you
          gave
        To Ralph, Vasey, Alastair, Biddy, John and
          me.

  As Mr. Sparrow wrote: " There is a great variety
of landscape in his poems: unlike most pastoral
poets, each of whom has his own ' Especial rural
scene '—Crabbe on the Suffolk coast, Cowper on
the banks of the Ouse, Barnes among the farms of
Dorsetshire—this poet is equally at home in the
most diverse surroundings."
  It is a long cry, for example, from the storm-
lashed coast of Cornwall to the timeless lassitude
of Southern Ireland, but the transition presents
Betjeman with not the slightest difficulty. Never
has the atmosphere of this lotus island, in which
time seems to stand still or rather to ebb slowly and
staunchlessly away, been more brilliantly captured
than in " Sunday in Ireland ". The country seems
to come before our eyes as we read, slumbering in its
torpid repose. Louis Macneice had written before:

    Look into your heart and you will find a County
    Sligo and a litter of chronicles and bones—

but Betjeman is more gentle in his approach:

    Bells are booming down the bohreens,
      White the mist along the grass.

Now the Julias, Maeves and Maureens
   Move between the fields to Mass.

     .   .   .   .

Stony seaboard, far and foreign,
   Stony hills poured over space,
Stony outcrop of the Burren,
   Stones in every fertile place,
Little fields with boulders dotted,
Grey-stone shoulders saffron-spotted,
Stone-walled cabins thatched with reeds,
Where a Stone Age people breeds
   The last of Europe's Stone Age race.

The poem comes to its end melancholy as the fine
rain that falls persistently upon the Irish fields:

Sheepswool, straw and droppings cover,
Graves of spinster, rake and lover,
Whose fantastic mausoleum
Sings its own seablown Te Deum,
   In and out the slipping slates.

It is another long jump from Eire to Henley-on-
Thames:

When shall I see the Thames again ?
The prow-promoted gems again,
   As beefy ATS
   Without their hats
Come shooting through the bridge ?
   And " cheerioh " and " cheeri-bye "
   Across the waste of waters die,
   And low the mists of evening lie
And lightly skims the midge.

The apparently effortless manner in which John Betjeman writes should deceive no one as to the intense care that goes into his craftsmanship, and its great metrical skill. Every word pulls its weight and there are no grace notes. He is also an admirable writer of blank verse which he finds easier than prose, and such is the fluency with which he writes in this form that he must exercise a constant discipline when using it. But at his best he is capable of lines like these which in their sustained beauty are comparable to anything written in that metre in the past or present. They occur in " Sunday Afternoon Service in St. Enodoc ":

Forced by the backwash, see the nearest wave
Rise to a wall of huge, translucent green
And crumble into spray along the top
Blown seaward by the land-breeze. Now she breaks
And in an arch of thunder plunges down
To burst and tumble, foam on top of foam.
Criss-crossing, baffled, sucked and shot again,
A waterfall of whiteness, down a rock,
Without a source but roller's furthest reach:
And tufts of sea-pink, high and dry for years,
Are flooded out of ledges, boulders seem
No bigger than a pebble washed about
In this tremendous tide.

Apart from blank verse Betjeman has experimented in many other difficult and complicated forms, and has seldom failed; we may take as an example of these the first stanza of his poem on Dr. Ramsden of Pembroke College, Oxford, which is a good example of metrical skill:

Dr. Ramsden cannot read the *Times* obituary to-day,
    He's dead.

Let monographs on silk worms by other people be
  Thrown away
  Unread
For he who best could understand and criticize
    them, he
  Lies clay
  In bed.

John Betjeman is not, I think, particularly fond
of making new acquaintances, but lavishes deep
affection upon old friends. Their deaths strike him
with a terrible impact, and reduce to despair a
nature already prone to bouts of depression. Here
we see him in yet another light, as the writer of
Elegies. It has always been a matter of surprise
to me that one of the finest and most moving of
these has attracted so little interest, and has escaped
the attention of anthologists. This was his poem
on the death of his contemporary and intimate
friend, the Marquess of Dufferin and Ava, Bracken-
bury Scholar at Balliol, a dark fascinating creature
who was killed fighting against the Japanese. The
elegy is of particular interest, for such was Betjeman's
intense grief at the loss of his friend, that for perhaps
the first time in his work he allows his own emotions
to become evident in the poetry. It is his normal
practice to adorn a poem with all the skill of which
he is capable, but to leave it to the reader to specu-
late as to what his inner feelings and motives in
writing it were:

  Friend of my youth, you are dead!
    and the long peal pours from the steeple
  Over this sunlit quad
    in our University City

And soaks in Headington stone.
　Motionless stand the pinnacles.

. . . .

Then there were people about.
　Each hour, like an Oxford archway,
Opened on long green lawns
　and distant unvisited buildings
And you my friend were explorer
　and so you remained to me always
Humorous, reckless, loyal—
　my kind, heavy-lidded companion.
Stop, oh many bells, stop
　pouring on roses and creeper
Your unremembering peal
　this hollow, unhallowed V.E. day,—
I am deaf to your notes and dead
　by a soldier's body in Burma.

It is impossible to write a note on John Betjeman's poetry without some reference to the abysmal depression sometimes apparent in it, and to his avowed terror of death. In this, if in no other respect, he resembles Dr. Johnson. There are those who say that he is a hypochondriac who creates these terrors of the dawn " when all the wheels of being slow ", Charcot's " Malade au petit morceau de papier ", but this is not true. It is a malaise of the soul against which his religious beliefs, strongly held, appear to offer no adequate shield. We shall search these poems in vain for any clue from him to the causes or nature of these dark passages. The poet is firmly behind his defences, and it is for the reader to make his own conjectures. He will find several such poems in Betjeman's *A Few Late*

Chrysanthemums, of which " The Cottage Hospital "
is a good example:

> Say in what Cottage Hospital
>   whose pale green walls resound
> With the tap upon polished parquet
>   of inflexible nurses' feet
> Shall I myself be lying
>   when they range the screens around ?
> And say shall I groan in dying,
>   as I twist the sweaty sheet ?
> Or gasp for breath uncrying,
>   as I feel my senses drown'd
> While the air is swimming with insects
>   and children play in the street ?

Let us also notice with what resentful skill he
describes the death-bed in " Remorse ":

> The nurse lays down her knitting and walks across
>   to her
> With quick professional eye she surveys the dead.
> Just one patient the less and little the loss to her,
>   Distantly tender she settles the shrunken head.

Another form of depression to which John
Betjeman is prone is a sense of physical inferiority.
This particular quirk, from which he derives maso-
chistic satisfaction, leads him to depict himself as
the crushed adorer of enormous tennis girls in whose
muscular arms he longs to crumple. These poems
are always extremely funny, and the poet usually
manages to introduce some disparaging reference to
his own physical appearance. I cannot say that
I am drawn towards the sort of amazons he depicts:

> Pam, I adore you, Pam, you great big mountainous
>   sports girl,

Whizzing them over the net, full of the strength
  of five:
That old Malvernian brother, you zephyr and khaki
    shorts girl,
        Although he's playing for Woking,
        Can't stand up
To your wonderful backhand drive.

To this category also, of course, belongs Miss Joan
Hunter Dunn, and the beefy enchantress whose
delights are lyrically extolled in " The Olympic
Girl ":

The sort of girl I like to see
Smiles down from her great height at me.
She stands in strong, athletic pose
And wrinkles her *retroussé* nose. . . .
Oh ! would I were her racket press'd
With hard excitement to her breast . . .
And banged against the bounding ball.
" Oh !   Plung ! " my tauten'd strings would call,
" Oh !   Plung ! my darling, break my strings
For you I will do brilliant things." . . .
And then, with what supreme caress,
You'ld tuck me up into my press.
Fair tigress of the tennis courts,
So short in sleeve and strong in shorts,
Little, alas, to you I mean,
For I am bald and old and green.

We have seen, then, that far from being the idolator
of ugliness driven by a perverse fancy towards the
suburban scene, he touches and illuminates life at
many different points.   Of this undeniable interest
in the suburbs I have already spoken and his

tenderness for them is surely evident in these lines from " Harrow-on-the-Hill ":

When melancholy Autumn comes to Wembley
And electric trains are lighted after tea
The poplars near the Stadium are trembly
With their tap and tap and whispering to me,
Like the sound of little breakers
Spreading out along the surf-line
When the estuary's filling
With the sea.

But here a warning needs to be issued. John Betjeman is not a ' funny ' poet, and resents being regarded as one, though he frequently writes supremely funny poems because prolonged solemnity is not in his nature. He does not write about the suburbs because he thinks them funny but because he likes them and knows their landscapes as he knows that of Essex or Cornwall, Ireland or the Thames Valley.

His interest in the suburbs should not blind us to Betjeman's horror of the vulgarity of modern life and the vandalism which has become parasitical upon it. In an age when much of the South Downs has been pock-marked by an obscene rash of jerry-built houses, and when one by one the elegant façades in London are torn down to give way to immense concrete boxes garish with fluorescent lighting, when even the Nash terraces are im-perilled, he stands for the small, the local, the kindly. He feels abhorrence for that form of modern taste which causes the old high-backed oak settees to be removed disdainfully from village inns, the stuffed fish in their glass cases consigned to the ash-heap, the moth-eaten otters' heads taken from the walls to be replaced by fumed oak and chromium-plated bars.

He detests modern urban public houses too, and he believes that such a gruesome décor attracts the clientèle it deserves, writing angrily about it in " Slough ":

> But spare the bald young clerks who add
> The profits of the stinking cad;
> It's not their fault that they are mad.
> They've tasted Hell.
>
> It's not their fault they do not know
> The birdsong from the radio,
> It's not their fault they often go
> To Maidenhead
>
> And talk of sport and makes of cars
> In various bogus-Tudor bars
> And daren't look up and see the stars
> But belch instead.

Few have done more to combat the encroach-ments of this form of progress with the squalor that is accessory to it than John Betjeman, and in the preservation of many an old building and graceful prospect whose rape was contemplated we may see his work. In " The Planster's Vision " we see Betjeman's hatred not only of desecration, but also of the new class of planners who are often responsible for its execution:

Cut down that timber! Bells, too many and strong . . .
Remove those cottages, a huddled throng!

Too many babies have been born in there,
Too many coffins, bumping down the stair,
Carried the old their garden paths along.

I have a Vision of the Future, chum,
    The workers' flats in fields of soya beans
        Tower up like silver pencils, score on score
And Surging Millions hear the Challenge come
    From microphones in communal canteens
        " No Right ! No Wrong ! All's perfect, ever-
            more."

And yet if, in spite of the hatred, Betjeman has
not on the whole succeeded as a satirist, it is only
because he is lacking in the cruelty and spite that
are inseparable from that art.

Some new verses included in this book from *Poems
in the Porch*, although Betjeman does not rate them
highly, will remind readers that he is also an admir-
able archæological and ecclesiastical poet.   On the
subject of ecclesiastical architecture his knowledge
is deep, from cathedrals to parish churches.   His
love of these village churches fills a great part of
his life, and his familiarity with them is extra-
ordinary.   It is a chastening experience to be told
the names and history of half a dozen within a
radius of twenty miles from where one has lived
since childhood and which one has never known.
His love for the Church of England is deep, but at
the same time intimate and homely, and as we read
we are almost aware of the musty smell of hassocks
and old hymn-books in the aisle.   It is partly the
love of architecture that makes him write with such
felicity about Oxford, that and the lilac and labur-
num in the Banbury Road, bergamot in the College

gardens, dragonflies skimming the green waters of Parsons Pleasure, and the ghost of Matthew Arnold.

Some have written of the great advancement as a poet made by Betjeman since those distant days at Oxford when he convulsed the more sophisticated undergraduates with " The 'Varsity Students' Rag ", to the present level of his performance. My own feeling is one of wonderment that such juvenilia should still appear as fresh and witty to me now as they did then, and to have defied the erosion of time.

Postscript 1970

Two further works of John Betjeman have been published since this Introduction was first printed —*Summoned by Bells*, a long autobiographical poem in blank verse, and *High and Low*, in which the poet returns to a number of favourite themes. The latter is included in this new collected edition. *Summoned by Bells* had an enthusiastic welcome, and found a wide audience, although a certain amount of hostile criticism was also forthcoming from the usual quarters. To sustain a description of his own life from childhood to the end of his Oxford days in blank verse was a formidable undertaking, and the poem is broken up by lyrics in the manner of Tennyson's *Princess*, which are effective in preventing the blank verse from developing a limp on its long journey. Perhaps the best parts of this poem are to be found, as usual, when the poet is writing of the places he loves most, Oxford and Cornwall. But his Oxford is that of the late 1920's, which Evelyn Waugh also described with glowing nostalgia in *Brideshead Revisited*, to the disgust of some ' progressive ' critics. John Betjeman's memories of

Oxford in *Summoned by Bells* are equally nostalgic, and evocative of a haven of leisured ease, which reminds one of Max Beerbohm's Oxford and Zuleika Dobson, and which must appear not only frivolous but also incomprehensible to the students of today —a warm and tender afterglow from a vanished age.

In *High and Low* Betjeman's heart seems to be most in his work when he is writing about Cornwall or Ireland, which has also, as we have seen, always exerted a strong spell upon him. Some readers and critics of *High and Low* have found in it an increased gloom and melancholy, and what appears to resemble closely a wallow in the atmosphere of the Men's Ward and the approach of a lonely death. These themes can be found in such poems as *Goodbye* and *Five o'Clock Shadow*. Those who are dispirited by them might remember that John Betjeman is a man of almost irritatingly robust health who, so far as I know, has not suffered a day's serious illness for the last thirty years.

Betjeman has had several brushes on committees with senior members of the Civil Service, in his efforts to avert acts of vandalism in town and country, and soon he formed a low opinion of the mental processes of even the most gifted Civil Servants. This intolerance may be wrong, but it has produced *Mortality*, one of the most effective poems in this collection:

The first-class brains of a senior civil servant
    Shiver and shatter and fall
As the steering column of his comfortable Humber
    Batters in the bony wall.
All those delicate little re-adjustments
    " On the one hand, if we proceed

With the *ad hoc* policy hitherto adapted
  To individual need . . .
On the other hand, too rigid an arrangement
  Might, of itself, perforce . . .
I would like to submit for the Minister's concurrence
  The following alternative course,
Subject to revision and reconsideration
  In the light our experience gains . . ."
And this had to happen at the corner where the by-
    pass
  Comes into Egham out of Staines.
That very near miss for an All Souls' Fellowship
  The recent compensation of a ' K '—
The first-class brains of a senior civil servant
  Are sweetbread on the road today.

COLLECTED POEMS

Death in Leamington

She died in the upstairs bedroom
    By the light of the ev'ning star
That shone through the plate glass window
    From over Leamington Spa.

Beside her the lonely crochet
    Lay patiently and unstirred,
But the fingers that would have work'd it
    Were dead as the spoken word.

And Nurse came in with the tea-things
    Breast high 'mid the stands and chairs—
But Nurse was alone with her own little soul,
    And the things were alone with theirs.

She bolted the big round window,
    She let the blinds unroll,
She set a match to the mantle,
    She covered the fire with coal.

And " Tea ! " she said in a tiny voice
  " Wake up !   It's nearly *five*."
Oh !   Chintzy, chintzy cheeriness,
  Half dead and half alive !

Do you know that the stucco is peeling ?
  Do you know that the heart will stop ?
From those yellow Italianate arches
  Do you hear the plaster drop ?

Nurse looked at the silent bedstead,
  At the gray, decaying face,
As the calm of a Leamington ev'ning
  Drifted into the place.

She moved the table of bottles
  Away from the bed to the wall;
And tiptoeing gently over the stairs
  Turned down the gas in the hall.

Hymn

The Church's Restoration
  In eighteen-eighty-three
Has left for contemplation
  Not what there used to be.
How well the ancient woodwork
  Looks round the Rect'ry hall,
Memorial of the good work
  Of him who plann'd it all.

He who took down the pew-ends
  And sold them anywhere
But kindly spared a few ends
  Work'd up into a chair.
O worthy persecution
  Of dust !   O hue divine !
O cheerful substitution,
  Thou varnishéd pitch-pine !

Church furnishing !   Church furnishing !
  Sing art and crafty praise !

3

He gave the brass for burnishing
  He gave the thick red baize,
He gave the new addition,
  Pull'd down the dull old aisle,
—To pave the sweet transition
  He gave th' encaustic tile.

Of marble brown and veinéd
  He did the pulpit make;
He order'd windows stainéd
  Light red and crimson lake.
Sing on, with hymns uproarious,
  Ye humble and aloof,
Look up ! and oh how glorious
  He has restored the roof !

The 'Varsity Students' Rag

I'm afraid the fellows in Putney rather wish they had
The social ease and manners of a 'varsity undergrad,
For tho' they're awf'lly decent and up to a lark as a rule
You want to have the 'varsity touch after a public school.

CHORUS:

> We had a rag at Monico's.   We had a rag at the Troc.,
>
> And the one we had at the Berkeley gave the customers
> quite a shock.
>
> Then we went to the Popular, and after that—oh my!
>
> I wish you'd seen the rag we had in the Grill Room at
> the Cri.

I started a rag in Putney at our Frothblower's Branch down
there;

We got in a damn'd old lorry and drove to Trafalgar Square;

And we each had a couple of toy balloons and made the hell
of a din,

And I saw a bobby at Parson's Green who looked like
running us in.

CHORUS: We, etc.

5

But that's nothing to the rag we had at the college the
other night;

We'd gallons and gallons of cider—and I got frightfully
tight.

And then we smash'd up ev'rything, and what was the
funniest part

We smashed some rotten old pictures which were priceless
works of art.

CHORUS: We, etc.

There's something about a 'varsity man that distinguishes
him from a cad:

You can tell by his tie and blazer he's a 'varsity undergrad,

And you know that he's always ready and up to a bit of a
lark,

With a toy balloon and a whistle and some cider after dark.

CHORUS: We, etc.

The City

Business men with awkward hips
And dirty jokes upon their lips,
And large behinds and jingling chains,
And riddled teeth and riddling brains,
And plump white fingers made to curl
Round some anaemic city girl,
And so lend colour to the lives
And old suspicions of their wives.

Young men who wear on office stools
The ties of minor public schools,
Each learning how to be a sinner
And tell " a good one " after dinner,
And so discover it is rather
Fun to go one more than father.
But father, son and clerk join up
To talk about the Football Cup.

An Eighteenth-Century Calvinistic Hymn

Thank God my Afflictions are such
　That I cannot lie down on my Bed,
And if I but take to my Couch
　I incessantly Vomit and Bleed.

I am not too sure of my Worth,
　Indeed it is tall as a Palm;
But what Fruits can it ever bring forth
　When Leprosy sits at the Helm ?

Though Torment's the Soul's Goal's Rewards
　The contrary's Proof of my Guilt,
While Dancing, Backgammon and Cards,
　Are among the worst Symptoms I've felt.

Oh ! I bless the good Lord for my Boils
　For my mental and bodily pains,
For without them my Faith all congeals
　And I'm doomed to HELL'S NE'ER-ENDING
　　　　　　　　　　　　　　FLAMES.

8

For Nineteenth-Century Burials

This cold weather
Carries so many old people away.
Quavering voices and blankets and breath
Go silent together.
The gentle fingers are touching to pray
Which crumple and straighten for Death.
These cold breezes
Carry the bells away on the air,
Stuttering tales of Gothic, and pass,
Catching new grave flowers into their hair,
Beating the chapel and red-coloured glass.

Camberley

I wonder whether you would make
A friend of Mrs. Kittiwake ?
Colonel Kittiwake, it's true,
Is not the sort of man for you.
I'll tell you how to get to know
Their cosy little bungalow.
When sunset gilds the Surrey pines
The fam'ly usually dines.
So later, in the Surrey dark,
Make for Poonah Punkah Park,
And by the monument to Clive
You'll come to Enniscorthy Drive,
Coolgreena is the last of all,
And mind the terrier when you call.

The drawing-room is done in pink
The other rooms are mauve, I think,
So when you see electric light
Behind pink curtains it's all right.

10

Knock gently, don't disturb the maid,
She's got to clear, and I'm afraid
That she is less inclined to take
The blame than Mrs. Kittiwake.

Croydon

In a house like that
    Your Uncle Dick was born;
Satchel on back he walked to Whitgift
    Every weekday morn.

Boys together in Coulsdon woodlands,
    Bramble-berried and steep,
He and his pals would look for spadgers
    Hidden deep.

The laurels are speckled in Marchmont Avenue
    Just as they were before,
But the steps are dusty that still lead up to
    Your Uncle Dick's front door.

Pear and apple in Croydon gardens
    Bud and blossom and fall,
But your Uncle Dick has left his Croydon
    Once for all.

12

Westgate-on-Sea

Hark, I hear the bells of Westgate,
  I will tell you what they sigh,
Where those minarets and steeples
  Prick the open Thanet sky.

Happy bells of eighteen-ninety,
  Bursting from your freestone tower !
Recalling laurel, shrubs and privet,
  Red geraniums in flower.

Feet that scamper on the asphalt
  Through the Borough Council grass,
Till they hide inside the shelter
  Bright with ironwork and glass,

Striving chains of ordered children
  Purple by the sea-breeze made,
Striving on to prunes and suet
  Past the shops on the Parade.

13

Some with wire around their glasses,
    Some with wire across their teeth,
Writhing frames for running noses
    And the drooping lip beneath.

Church of England bells of Westgate !
    On this balcony I stand,
White the woodwork wriggles round me,
    Clock towers rise on either hand.

For me in my timber arbour
    You have one more message yet,
" Plimsolls, plimsolls in the summer,
    Oh goloshes in the wet ! "

The Wykehamist

(To Randolph Churchill, but not about him.)

Broad of Church and broad of mind,
Broad before and broad behind,
A keen ecclesiologist,
A rather dirty Wykehamist.
'Tis not for us to wonder why
He wears that curious knitted tie;
We should not cast reflections on
The very slightest kind of don.
We should not giggle as we like
At his appearance on his bike;
It's something to become a bore,
And more than that, at twenty-four.
It's something too to know your wants
And go full pelt for Norman fonts.
Just now the chestnut trees are dark
And full with shadow in the park,
And " six o'clock ! " St. Mary calls
Above the mellow college walls.

15

The evening stretches arms to twist
And captivate her Wykehamist.
But not for him these autumn days,
He shuts them out with heavy baize;
He gives his Ovaltine a stir
And nibbles at a " petit beurre ",
And, satisfying fleshy wants,
He settles down to Norman fonts.

The Sandemanian Meeting-House
in Highbury Quadrant

On roaring iron down the Holloway Road
  The red trams and the brown trams pour,
And little each yellow-faced jolted load
  Knows of the fast-shut grained oak door.

From Canonbury, Dalston and Mildmay Park
  The old North London shoots in a train
To the long black platform, gaslit and dark,
  Oh Highbury Station once and again.

Steam or electric, little they care,
  Yellow brick terrace or terra-cotta hall,
White-wood sweet shop or silent square,
  That the LORD OF THE SCRIPTURES IS LORD OF ALL.

Away from the barks and the shouts and the greetings,
  Psalm-singing over and love-lunch done,
Listening to the Bible in their room for meetings,
  Old Sandemanians are hidden from the sun.

17

The Arrest of Oscar Wilde at the Cadogan Hotel

He sipped at a weak hock and seltzer
    As he gazed at the London skies
Through the Nottingham lace of the curtains
    Or was it his bees-winged eyes ?

To the right and before him Pont Street
    Did tower in her new built red,
As hard as the morning gaslight
    That shone on his unmade bed,

" I want some more hock in my seltzer,
    And Robbie, please give me your hand—
Is this the end or beginning ?
    How can I understand ?

" So you've brought me the latest *Yellow Book*:
    And Buchan has got in it now:
Approval of what is approved of
    Is as false as a well-kept vow.

" More hock, Robbie—where is the seltzer ?
  Dear boy, pull again at the bell !
They are all little better than *cretins*,
  Though this *is* the Cadogan Hotel.

" One astrakhan coat is at Willis's—
  Another one's at the Savoy:
Do fetch my morocco portmanteau,
  And bring them on later, dear boy."

A thump, and a murmur of voices—
  (" Oh why must they make such a din ? ")
As the door of the bedroom swung open
  And TWO PLAIN CLOTHES POLICEMEN came in:

" Mr. Woilde, we 'ave come for tew take yew
  Where felons and criminals dwell:
We must ask yew tew leave with us quoietly
  For this *is* the Cadogan Hotel."

He rose, and he put down *The Yellow Book*.
  He staggered—and, terrible-eyed,
He brushed past the palms on the staircase
  And was helped to a hansom outside.

Distant View of a Provincial Town

Beside those spires so spick and span
    Against an unencumbered sky
The old Great Western Railway ran
    When someone different was I.

St. Aidan's with the prickly nobs
    And iron spikes and coloured tiles—
Where Auntie Maud devoutly bobs
    In those enriched vermilion aisles:

St. George's where the mattins bell
    But rarely drowned the trams for prayer—
No Popish sight or sound or smell
    Disturbed that gas-invaded air:

St. Mary's where the Rector preached
    In such a jolly friendly way
On cricket, football, things that reached
    The simple life of every day:

And that United Benefice
  With entrance permanently locked,—
How Gothic, grey and sad it is
  Since Mr. Grogley was unfrocked !

The old Great Western Railway shakes
  The old Great Western Railway spins—
The old Great Western Railway makes
  Me very sorry for my sins.

Slough

Come, friendly bombs, and fall on Slough
It isn't fit for humans now,
There isn't grass to graze a cow
    Swarm over, Death !

Come, bombs, and blow to smithereens
Those air-conditioned, bright canteens,
Tinned fruit, tinned meat, tinned milk, tinned beans
    Tinned minds, tinned breath.

Mess up the mess they call a town—
A house for ninety-seven down
And once a week a half-a-crown
    For twenty years,

And get that man with double chin
Who'll always cheat and always win,
Who washes his repulsive skin
    In women's tears,

And smash his desk of polished oak
And smash his hands so used to stroke
And stop his boring dirty joke
    And make him yell.

But spare the bald young clerks who add
The profits of the stinking cad;
It's not their fault that they are mad,
    They've tasted Hell.

It's not their fault they do not know
The birdsong from the radio,
It's not their fault they often go
    To Maidenhead

And talk of sports and makes of cars
In various bogus Tudor bars
And daren't look up and see the stars
    But belch instead.

In labour-saving homes, with care
Their wives frizz out peroxide hair
And dry it in synthetic air
    And paint their nails.

Come, friendly bombs, and fall on Slough
To get it ready for the plough.
The cabbages are coming now;
    The earth exhales.

Clash went the Billiard Balls

Clash went the billiard balls in the Clerkenwell Social Saloon.

Shut up the shutters and turn down the gas they'll be
calling the coppers in soon.

Goodnight, Alf !

Goodnight, Bert !

Goodnight, Mrs. Gilligan !

Rain in the archway, no trams in the street.

COP COP

Cop on the cobbleway

Quick little ladylike feet

" 'Ard luck, ain't got a gentleman ? "

" Not on a night like this, sweet "

" The Red Lion, Myddleton, all the 'ole lot of 'em

Shut but a light in The Star

Counting the coppers to see what they've got of 'em

Glistening wet in the bar

32, 34, 36, 38, Gaskin's not back with 'is tart

Left the 'all door open gives 'imself airs 'e does

Thinks 'imself too bloody smart

25

Gas on in the 'all and it's *we've* got to pay for it
Damn these old stairs and this bug-ridden panelling
See 'im to-morrow what *'e's* got to say for it
Get on the bed there and start."

Love in a Valley

Take me, Lieutenant, to that Surrey homestead !
    Red comes the winter and your rakish car,
Red among the hawthorns, redder than the hawberries
    And trails of old man's nuisance, and noisier far.
Far, far below me roll the Coulsdon woodlands,
    White down the valley curves the living rail,[1]
Tall, tall, above me, olive spike the pinewoods,
    Olive against blue-black, moving in the gale.

Deep down the drive go the cushioned rhododendrons,
    Deep down, sand deep, drives the heather root,
Deep the spliced timber barked around the summer-house,
    Light lies the tennis-court, plantain underfoot.
What a winter welcome to what a Surrey homestead !
    Oh ! the metal lantern and white enamelled door !
Oh ! the spread of orange from the gas-fire on the carpet !
    Oh ! the tiny patter, sandalled footsteps on the floor !

[1] Southern Electric 25 mins.

Fling wide the curtains !—that's a Surrey sunset
  Low down the line sings the Addiscombe train,
Leaded are the windows lozenging the crimson,
  Drained dark the pines in resin-scented rain.
Portable Lieutenant ! they carry you to China
  And me to lonely shopping in a brilliant arcade;
Firm hand, fond hand, switch the giddy engine !
  So for us a last time is bright light made.

An Impoverished Irish Peer

Within that parsonage
There is a personage
Who owns a mortgage
    On his Lordship's land,
On his fine plantations,
Well speculated,
With groves of beeches
    On either hand—
On his ten ton schooner
Upon Loch Gowna,
And the silver birches
    Along the land—
Where the little pebbles
Do sing like trebles
As the waters bubble
    Upon the strand—

On his gateway olden
Of plaster moulded

And his splendid carriage way
    To Castle Grand,
(They've been aquatinted
For a book that's printed
And even wanted
    In far England)
His fine saloons there
Would make you swoon, sir,
And each surrounded
    By a gilded band—
And 'tis there Lord Ashtown
Lord Trimlestown and
Clonmore's Lord likewise
    Are entertained.

As many flunkeys
As Finnea has donkeys
Are there at all times
    At himself's command.
Though he doesn't pay them
They all obey him
And would sure die for him
    If he waved his hand;
Yet if His Lordship

Comes for to worship
At the Holy Table
    To take his stand,
Though humbly kneeling
There's no fair dealing
And no kind feeling
    In the parson's hand.
Preaching of Liberty
Also of Charity
In the grand high pulpit
    To see him stand,
You'ld think that personage
In that parsonage
Did own no mortgage
    On His Lordship's land.

Our Padre

Our padre is an old sky pilot,
  Severely now they've clipped his wings
But still the flagstaff in the Rect'ry garden
  Points to Higher Things.

Still he has got a hearty handshake;
  Still he wears his medals and a stole;
His voice would reach to Heaven, *and* make
  The Rock of Ages Roll.

He's too sincere to join the high church
  Worshipping idols for the Lord,
And, though the lowest church is my church,
  Our padre's Broad.

Our padre is an old sky pilot,
  He's tied a reef knot round my heart,
We'll be rocked up to Heaven on a rare old tune—
  Come on—take part !

(*Sung*) Pull for the shore, sailor, pull for the shore !

Heed not the raging billow, bend to the oar !

Bend to the oar before the padre !

Proud, with the padre rowing stroke !

Good old padre ! God for the services !

Row like smoke !

Exchange of Livings

Lines suggested by an advertisement in *The Guardian* (the Broad Church newspaper).

The church was locked, so I went to the incumbent—

the incumbent enjoying a supine incumbency—

a tennis court, a summerhouse, deckchairs by the walnut tree

and only the hum of the bees in the rockery.

" May I have the keys of the church, your incumbency ? "

" Yes, my dear sir, as a moderate churchman,

I am willing to exchange: light Sunday duty:
nice district: pop 149: eight hundred per annum:

no extremes: A and M: bicyclist essential:
same income expected."

" I think I'm the man that you want, your incumbency.

Here's my address when I'm not on my bicycle, poking
about for recumbent stone effigies—

14, Mount Ephraim, Cheltenham, Glos:

Rector St. George-in-the-Rolling Pins, Cripplegate:

non resident pop in the City of London:

eight fifty per annum (but verger an asset):

willing to exchange (no extremes) for incumbency,

similar income, but closer to residence."

34

Undenominational

Undenominational
   But still the church of God
He stood in his conventicle
   And ruled it with a rod.

Undenominational
   The walls around him rose,
The lamps within their brackets shook
   To hear the hymns he chose.

" Glory " " Gospel " " Russell Place "
   " Wrestling Jacob " " Rock "
" Saffron Walden " " Safe at Home "
   " Dorking " " Plymouth Dock "

I slipped about the chalky lane
   That runs without the park,
I saw the lone conventicle
   A beacon in the dark.

Revival ran along the hedge
And made my spirit whole
When steam was on the window panes
And glory in my soul.

City

When the great bell
BOOMS over the Portland stone urn, and
From the carved cedar wood
Rises the odour of incense,
I SIT DOWN
In St. Botolph Bishopsgate Churchyard
And wait for the spirit of my grandfather
Toddling along from the Barbican.

A Hike on the Downs

" Yes, rub some soap upon your feet !
   We'll hike round Winchester for weeks—
Like ancient Britons—just we two—
   Or more perhaps like ancient Greeks.

" You take your pipe—that will impress
   Your strength on anyone who passes;
I'll take my *Plautus* (*non purgatus*)
   And both my pairs of horn-rimmed glasses.

" I've got my first, and now I know
   What life is and what life contains—
For, being just a first year man
   You don't meet all the first-class brains.

" Objectively, our Common Room
   Is like a small Athenian State—
Except for Lewis: he's all right
   But do you think he's *quite* first rate ?

38

Hampshire mentality is low,
    And that is why they stare at us.
Yes, here's the earthwork—but it's dark;
    We may as well return by bus."

Dorset

Rime Intrinsica, Fontmell Magna, Sturminster Newton and
Melbury Bubb,

Whist upon whist upon whist upon whist drive, in Institute,
Legion and Social Club.

Horny hands that hold the aces which this morning held
the plough—

While Tranter Reuben, T. S. Eliot, H. G. Wells and Edith
Sitwell lie in Mellstock Churchyard now.

Lord's Day bells from Bingham's Melcombe, Iwerne Minster,
Shroton, Plush,

Down the grass between the beeches, mellow in the evening
hush.

Gloved the hands that hold the hymn-book, which this
morning milked the cow—

While Tranter Reuben, Mary Borden, Brian Howard and
Harold Acton lie in Mellstock Churchyard now.

Light's abode, celestial Salem ! Lamps of evening, smelling
strong,

Gleaming on the pitch-pine, waiting, almost empty even-
song:

From the aisles each window smiles on grave and grass and
                                                yew-tree bough—

While Tranter Reuben, Gordon Selfridge, Edna Best and
        Thomas Hardy lie in Mellstock Churchyard now.

   NOTE : *The names in the last lines of these stanzas
are put in not out of malice or satire but merely for
their euphony.*

Calvinistic Evensong

The six bells stopped, and in the dark I heard
Cold silence wait the Calvinistic word;
For Calvin now the soft oil lamps are lit
Hands on their hymnals six old women sit.
Black gowned and sinister, he now appears
Curate-in-charge of aged parish fears.
Let, unaccompanied, that psalm begin
Which deals most harshly with the fruits of sin !
Boy ! pump the organ ! let the anthem flow
With promise for the chosen saints below !
Pregnant with warning the globed elm trees wait
Fresh coffin-wood beside the churchyard gate.
And that mauve hat three cherries decorate
Next week shall topple from its trembling perch
While wet fields reek like some long empty church.

Exeter

The doctor's intellectual wife
   Sat under the ilex tree
The Cathedral bells pealed over the wall
   But never a bell heard she
And the sun played shadowgraphs on her book
   Which was writ by A. Huxléy.

Once those bells, those Exeter bells
   Called her to praise and pray
By pink, acacia-shaded walls
   Several times a day
To Wulfric's altar and riddel posts
   While the choir sang Stanford in A.

The doctor jumps in his Morris car,
   The surgery door goes bang,
Clash and whirr down Colleton Crescent,
   Other cars all go hang
My little bus is enough for us—
   Till a tram-car bell went clang.

43

They brought him in by the big front door
    And a smiling corpse was he;
On the dining-room table they laid him out
    Where the *Bystanders* used to be—
The Tatler, The Sketch and *The Bystander*
    For the canons' wives to see.

Now those bells, those Exeter bells
    Call her to praise and pray
By pink, acacia-shaded walls
    Several times a day
To Wulfric's altar and riddel posts
    And the choir sings Stanford in A.

Death of King George V

"New King arrives in his capital by air . . ,"
Daily Newspaper.

Spirits of well-shot woodcock, partridge, snipe
  Flutter and bear him up the Norfolk sky:
In that red house in a red mahogany book-case
  The stamp collection waits with mounts long dry.

The big blue eyes are shut which saw wrong clothing
  And favourite fields and coverts from a horse;
Old men in country houses hear clocks ticking
  Over thick carpets with a deadened force;

Old men who never cheated, never doubted,
  Communicated monthly, sit and stare
At the new suburb stretched beyond the run-way
  Where a young man lands hatless from the air.

The Heart of Thomas Hardy

The heart of Thomas Hardy flew out of Stinsford churchyard
A little thumping fig, it rocketed over the elm trees.
Lighter than air it flew straight to where its Creator
Waited in golden nimbus, just as in eighteen sixty,
Hardman and son of Brum had depicted Him in the chancel.
Slowly out of the grass, slitting the mounds in the centre
Riving apart the roots, rose the new covered corpses
Tess and Jude and His Worship, various unmarried mothers,
Woodmen, cutters of turf, adulterers, church restorers,
Turning aside the stones thump on the upturned churchyard.
Soaring over the elm trees slower than Thomas Hardy,
Weighted down with a Conscience, now for the first time
fleshly

Taking form as a growth hung from the feet like a sponge-
bag.

There, in the heart of the nimbus, twittered the heart of
Hardy

There, on the edge of the nimbus, slowly revolved the
corpses

Radiating around the twittering heart of Hardy,
Slowly started to turn in the light of their own Creator
Died away in the night as frost will blacken a dahlia.

Suicide on Junction Road Station after Abstention from Evening Communion in North London

With the roar of the gas my heart gives a shout—
  To Jehovah Tsidkenu the praise !
Bracket and bracket go blazon it out
  In this Evangelical haze !

Jehovah Jireh ! the arches ring,
  The Mintons glisten, and grand
Are the surpliced boys as they sweetly sing
  On the threshold of glory land.

Jehovah Nisi ! from Tufnell Park,
  Five minutes to Junction Road,
Through grey brick Gothic and London dark,
  And my sins, a fearful load.

Six on the upside ! six on the down side !
  One gaslight in the Booking Hall
And a thousand sins on this lonely station—
  What shall I do with them all ?

The Flight from Bootle

Lonely in the Regent Palace,
   Sipping her " Banana Blush ",
Lilian lost sight of Alice
   In the honey-coloured rush.

Settled down at last from Bootle,
   Alice whispered, " Just a min,
While I pop upstairs and rootle
   For another safety pin."

Dreamy from the band pavilion
   Drops of the *Immortal Hour*
Fell around the lonely Lilian
   Like an ineffectual shower.

Half an hour she sat and waited
   In the honey-coloured lounge
Till she with herself debated,
   " Time for me to go and scrounge ! "

Time enough ! or not enough time !
   Lilian, you wait in vain;
Alice will not have a rough time,
   Nor be quite the same again.

Public House Drunk

Bass	Turn again, Higginson,
Treble	*thrice Mayor of London !*
Bass	Stretch the bow of your bells,
Treble	*St. Mary's steeple !*
Bass	Finsbury, Highbury,
Treble	*you are all undone !*
Bass	Moorfields and Cripplegate,
Treble	*wake up your people !*
Bass	Saint Andrew Undershaft,
Treble	*Saint Andrew Hubbard,*
Bass	Saint Catherine Coleman,
Treble	*Saint Botolph, Saint Bride's*
Bass	Where are your registers ?
Treble	*In vestry cupboard*
Bass	Look him up, Higginson,
Treble	*find where he hides !*
Bass	Out of the Jew's Harp House
Treble	*Old Mother Redcap*

Bass	Turn down the gas again
Treble	*—gas again, Glory !*
Bass	Clean up the bar in the
Treble	*wake of that madcap*
Bass	Lord Mayor of London ! Oh
Treble	*Lord what a story !*

Bass	Hold him down, Higginson !
Treble	*send for the beadles !*
Bass	" Fourteen, Macaulay street
Treble	*Bromley-by-Bow*
Bass	Represents pen-nibs
Treble	*steel holders and needles*
Bass	For the Office Equipment
Treble	*Efficiency Co."*

Cheltenham

Floruit, floret, floreat !
  Cheltonia's children cry.
I composed those lines when a summer wind
  Was blowing the elm leaves dry,
And we were seventy-six for seven
  And they had C. B. Fry.

Shall I forget the warm marquee
  And the general's wife so soon,
When my son's colleger[1] acted as tray
  For an ice and a macaroon,
And distant carriages jingled through
  The stuccoed afternoon ?

Floruit.   Yes, the Empire Map
  Cheltonia's sons have starred.
Floret.   Still the stream goes on
  Of soldier, brusher[2] and bard.
Floreat.   While behind the limes
  Lengthens the Promenade.

[1] Mortar board.   [2] Schoolmaster.

A Shropshire Lad

N.B.—This should be recited with a Midland accent.
Captain Webb, the swimmer and a relation of Mary Webb by marriage, was born at Dawley in an industrial district in Salop.

The gas was on in the Institute,[1]

    The flare was up in the gym,

A man was running a mineral line,

    A lass was singing a hymn,

When Captain Webb the Dawley man,

    Captain Webb from Dawley,

Came swimming along the old canal

    That carried the bricks to Lawley.

        Swimming along—

        Swimming along—

        Swimming along from Severn,

And paying a call at Dawley Bank while swimming along
                            to Heaven.

The sun shone low on the railway line

    And over the bricks and stacks,

[1] " The Institute was radiant with gas." Ch. XIX, *Boyhood.* A novel in verse by Rev. E. E. Bradford, D.D.

And in at the upstairs windows
   Of the Dawley houses' backs,
When we saw the ghost of Captain Webb,
   Webb in a water sheeting,
Come dripping along in a bathing dress
   To the Saturday evening meeting.
      Dripping along—
      Dripping along—
      To the Congregational Hall;
Dripping and still he rose over the sill and faded away in a
                                        wall.

There wasn't a man in Oakengates
   That hadn't got hold of the tale,
And over the valley in Ironbridge,
   And round by Coalbrookdale,
How Captain Webb the Dawley man,
   Captain Webb from Dawley,
Rose rigid and dead from the old canal
   That carries the bricks to Lawley.
      Rigid and dead—
      Rigid and dead—
      To the Saturday congregation,
Paying a call at Dawley Bank on his way to his destination.

Upper Lambourne

Up the ash-tree climbs the ivy,
　　Up the ivy climbs the sun,
With a twenty-thousand pattering
　　Has a valley breeze begun,
Feathery ash, neglected elder,
　　Shift the shade and make it run—

Shift the shade toward the nettles,
　　And the nettles set it free
To streak the stained Carrara headstone
　　Where, in nineteen-twenty-three,
He who trained a hundred winners
　　Paid the Final Entrance Fee.

Leathery limbs of Upper Lambourne,
　　Leathery skin from sun and wind,
Leathery breeches, spreading stables,
　　Shining saddles left behind—
To the down the string of horses
　　Moving out of sight and mind.

Feathery ash in leathery Lambourne
  Waves above the sarsen stone,
And Edwardian plantations
  So coniferously moan
As to make the swelling downland,
  Far-surrounding, seem their own.

Pot Pourri from a Surrey Garden

Miles of pram in the wind and Pam in the gorse track,
  Coco-nut smell of the broom, and a packet of Weights
Press'd in the sand.   The thud of a hoof on a horse-track—
    A horse-riding horse for a horse-track—
    Conifer county of Surrey approached
  Through remarkable wrought-iron gates.

Over your boundary now, I wash my face in a bird-bath,
  Then which path shall I take ? that over there by the
                                                    pram ?
Down by the pond ! or—yes, I will take the slippery third
                                                    path,
    Trodden away with gym shoes,
    Beautiful fir-dry alley that leads
  To the bountiful body of Pam.

Pam, I adore you, Pam, you great big mountainous sports
                                                    girl,
  Whizzing them over the net, full of the strength of five:
That old Malvernian brother, you zephyr and khaki shorts
                                                    girl,

Although he's playing for Woking,
　　Can't stand up
To your wonderful backhand drive.

See the strength of her arm, as firm and hairy as Hendren's;
　　See the size of her thighs, the pout of her lips as, cross,
And full of a pent-up strength, she swipes at the rhododen-
　　　　　　　　　　　　　　　　　　　　　　drons,
　　　　Lucky the rhododendrons,
　　　　And flings her arrogant love-lock
　　Back with a petulant toss.

Over the redolent pinewoods, in at the bathroom casement,
　　One fine Saturday, Windlesham bells shall call:
Up the Butterfield aisle rich with Gothic enlacement,
　　　　Licensed now for embracement,
　　　　Pam and I, as the organ
　　Thunders over you all.

Holy Trinity, Sloane Street
MCMVII

An Acolyte singeth

Light six white tapers with the Flame of Art,
Send incense wreathing to the lily flowers,
And, with your cool hands white,
Swing the warm censer round my bruised heart,
Drop, dove-grey eyes, your penitential showers
On this pale acolyte.

A cofirmandus continueth

The tall red house soars upward to the stars,
The doors are chased with sardonyx and gold,
And in the long white room
Thin drapery draws backward to unfold
Cadogan Square between the window-bars
And Whistler's mother knitting in the gloom.

The Priest endeth

How many hearts turn Motherward to-day ?
(Red roses faint not on your twining stems !)

Bronze triptych doors unswing !

Wait, restive heart, wait, rounded lips, to pray,

Mid beaten copper interset with gems

Behold !   Behold ! your King !

On Seeing an Old Poet in the Café Royal

I saw him in the Café Royal.
  Very old and very grand.
Modernistic shone the lamplight
  There in London's fairyland.
" Devilled chicken.   Devilled whitebait.
  Devil if I understand.

Where is Oscar ?   Where is Bosie ?
  Have I seen that man before ?
And the old one in the corner,
  Is it really Wratislaw ? "
Scent of Tutti-Frutti-Sen-Sen
  And cheroots upon the floor.

An Incident in the Early Life of Ebenezer Jones, Poet, 1828

" WE were together at a well-known boarding-school
of that day (1828), situated at the foot of Highgate
Hill, and presided over by a dissenting minister, the
Rev. John Bickerdike. . . .

We were together, though not on the same form;
and on a hot summer afternoon, with about fifty
other boys, were listlessly conning our tasks in a
large schoolroom built out from the house, which
made a cover for us to play under when it was wet.
Up the ladder-like stairs from the playground a
lurcher dog had strayed into the schoolroom, panting
with the heat, his tongue lolling out with thirst.
The choleric usher who presided, and was detested
by us for his tyranny, seeing this, advanced down
the room. Enraged at our attention being dis-
tracted from our tasks, he dragged the dog to the top
of the stairs, and there lifted him bodily up with the
evident intention—and we had known him do
similar things—of hurling the poor creature to the
bottom.

' YOU SHALL NOT ! ' rang through the room, as
little Ebby, so exclaiming at the top of his voice,
rushed with kindling face to the spot from among
all the boys—some of them twice his age.

But even while the words passed his lips, the
heavy fall was heard, and the sound seemed to
travel through his listening form and face, as, with

62

a strange look of anguish in one so young, he stood still, threw up his arms, and burst into an uncontrollable passion of tears.

With a coarse laugh at this, the usher led him back by his ear to the form; and there he sat, long after his sobbing had subsided, like one dazed and stunned." (*From an account of his brother by Sumner Jones in the 1879 re-issue of Ebenezer Jones's " Studies of Sensation and Event ".*)

The lumber of a London-going dray,
The still-new stucco on the London clay,
Hot summer silence over Holloway.

Dissenting chapels, tea-bowers, lovers' lairs,
Neat new-built villas, ample Grecian squares,
Remaining orchards ripening Windsor pears.

Hot silence where the older mansions hide
On Highgate Hill's thick elm-encrusted side,
And Pancras, Hornsey, Islington divide.

June's hottest silence where the hard rays strike
Yon hill-foot house, window and wall alike,
School of the Reverend Mr. Bickerdike,

For sons of Saints, blest with this world's possessions
(Seceders from the Protestant Secessions),
Good grounding in the more genteel professions.

63

A lurcher dog, which draymen kick and pass
Tongue lolling, thirsty over shadeless grass,
Leapt up the playground ladder to the class.

The godly usher left his godly seat,
His skin was prickly in the ungodly heat,
The dog lay panting at his godly feet.

The milkman on the road stood staring in,
The playground nettles nodded " Now begin "—
And Evil waited, quivering, for sin.

He lifted it and not a word he spoke,
His big hand tightened.   Could he make it choke
He trembled, sweated, and his temper broke.

" YOU SHALL NOT ! " clear across to Highgate Hill
A boy's voice sounded.   Creaking forms were still.
The cat jumped slowly from the window sill.

" YOU SHALL NOT ! " flat against the summer sun,
Hard as the hard sky frowning over one,
Gloat, little boys ! enjoy the coming fun !

" GOD DAMNS A CUR.   I AM, I AM HIS WORD ! "
He flung it, flung it and it never stirred,
" You shall not !—shall not ! " ringing on unheard.

Blind desolation ! bleeding, burning rod !
Big, bull-necked Minister of Calvin's God !
Exulting milkman, redfaced, shameless clod,

Look on and jeer !   Not Satan's thunder-quake
Can cause the mighty walls of Heaven to shake
As now they do, to hear a boy's heart break.

Trebetherick

We used to picnic where the thrift
    Grew deep and tufted to the edge;
We saw the yellow foam-flakes drift
    In trembling sponges on the ledge
Below us, till the wind would lift
    Them up the cliff and o'er the hedge.
Sand in the sandwiches, wasps in the tea,
Sun on our bathing-dresses heavy with the wet,
Squelch of the bladder-wrack waiting for the sea,
Fleas round the tamarisk, an early cigarette.

From where the coastguard houses stood
    One used to see, below the hill,
The lichened branches of a wood
    In summer silver-cool and still;
And there the Shade of Evil could
    Stretch out at us from Shilla Mill.
Thick with sloe and blackberry, uneven in the light,

Lonely ran the hedge, the heavy meadow was remote,
The oldest part of Cornwall was the wood as black as night,   .
And the pheasant and the rabbit lay torn open at the throat.

But when a storm was at its height,
    And feathery slate was black in rain,
And tamarisks were hung with light
    And golden sand was brown again,
Spring tide and blizzard would unite
    And sea came flooding up the lane.
Waves full of treasure then were roaring up the beach,
Ropes round our mackintoshes, waders warm and dry,
We waited for the wreckage to come swirling into reach,
Ralph, Vasey, Alastair, Biddy, John and I.

Then roller into roller curled
    And thundered down the rocky bay,
And we were in a water-world
    Of rain and blizzard, sea and spray,
And one against the other hurled
    We struggled round to Greenaway.
Blesséd be St. Enodoc, blesséd be the wave,
Blesséd be the springy turf, we pray, pray to thee,
Ask for our children all the happy days you gave
To Ralph, Vasey, Alastair, Biddy, John and me.

Oxford : Sudden Illness at the Bus-stop

At the time of evening when cars run sweetly,
  Syringas blossom by Oxford gates.
In her evening velvet with a rose pinned neatly
  By the distant bus-stop a don's wife waits.

From that wide bedroom with its two branched lighting
  Over her looking-glass, up or down,
When sugar was short and the world was fighting
  She first appeared in that velvet gown.

What forks since then have been slammed in places ?
  What peas turned out from how many a tin ?
From plate-glass windows how many faces
  Have watched professors come hobbling in ?

Too much, too many ! so fetch the doctor,
  This dress has grown such a heavier load
Since Jack was only a Junior Proctor,
  And rents were lower in Rawlinson Road.

Group Life: Letchworth

Tell me Pippididdledum,
   Tell me how the children are.
Working each for weal of all
   After what you said.
Barry's on the common far
   Pedalling the Kiddie Kar.
Ann has had a laxative
   And Alured is dead.
Sympathy is stencilling
   Her decorative leatherwork,
Wilfred's learned a folk-tune for
   The Morris Dancers' band.
I have my ex-Service man and
   Mamie's done a lino-cut.
And Charlie's in the *kinderbank*
   A-kicking up the sand.
Wittle-tittle, wittle-tittle
   Toodle-oodle ducky birds,
What a lot my dicky chicky

Tiny tots have done.
Wouldn't it be jolly now,
    To take our Aertex panters off
And have a jolly tumble in
    The jolly, jolly sun ?

Bristol and Clifton

" Yes, I was only sidesman here when last
You came to Evening Communion.
But now I have retired from the bank
I have more leisure time for church finance.
We moved into a somewhat larger house
Than when you knew us in Manilla Road.
This is the window to my lady wife.
You cannot see it now, but in the day
The greens and golds are truly wonderful."

" How very sad.   I do not mean about
The window, but I mean about the death
Of Mrs. Battlecock.   When did she die ? "

" Two years ago when we had just moved in
To Pembroke Road.   I rather fear the stairs
And basement kitchen were too much for her—
Not that, of course, she did the servants' work—
But supervising servants all the day
Meant quite a lot of climbing up and down."

71

"How very sad.   Poor Mrs. Battlecock."
" ' The glory that men do lives after them,' [1]
And so I gave this window in her name.
It's executed by a Bristol firm;
The lady artist who designed it, made
The figure of the lady on the left
Something like Mrs. Battlecock."
"How nice."

                "Yes, was it not ?   We had
A stained glass window on the stairs at home,
In Pembroke Road.   But not so good as this.
This window is the glory of the church
At least I think so—and the unstained oak
Looks very chaste beneath it.   When I gave
The oak, that brass inscription on your right
Commemorates the fact, the Dorcas Club
Made these blue kneelers, though we do not kneel:
We leave that to the Roman Catholics."
"How very nice, indeed.   How very nice."

"Seeing I have some knowledge of finance
Our kind Parochial Church Council made

        [1] Shakespeare, of course.

Me People's Warden, and I'm glad to say
That our collections are still keeping up.
The chancel has been flood-lit, and the stove
Which used to heat the church was obsolete.
So now we've had some radiators fixed
Along the walls and eastward of the aisles;
This last I thought of lest at any time
A Ritualist should be inducted here
And want to put up altars.   He would find
The radiators inconvenient.
Our only ritual here is with the Plate;
I think we make it dignified enough.
I take it up myself, and afterwards,
Count the Collection on the vestry safe."

" Forgive me, aren't we talking rather loud ?
I think I see a woman praying there."
" Praying ?   The service is all over now
And here's the verger waiting to turn out
The lights and lock the church up.   She cannot
Be Loyal Church of England.   Well, good-bye.
Time flies.   I must be going.   Come again.
There are some pleasant people living here.
I know the Inskips very well indeed."

Sir John Piers

OH! BOLD BAD BARONET
YOU NEED NO CORONET
YOU SIGN YOUR WARRANT WITH
A BLOODY HAND.

INTRODUCTION

" In 1807, Sir John Piers, the last of the name who resided in Tristernagh, and who was a gambler, duellist, and spendthrift, was a schoolfellow of the patriot, Lord Cloncurry. Shortly after the marriage of that nobleman, Piers, who shared his hospitality, and even received pecuniary aid from him, made a diabolical wager to ruin for life the happiness of the wedded pair. Mr. W. J. Fitzpatrick, the able biographer of Lord Cloncurry, says: '. . . A more unlikely person than Lady Cloncurry to prove unfaithful to him she had vowed to love, honour and obey, did not, perhaps, exist in Christendom. Can it be believed that such was the character which Sir John Piers resolved by every art of hell to wither and destroy ? A bet, or agreement, as we have heard, was entered into between the monster and some kindred spirit, that in the event of the utter and complete ruin of Lord and Lady Cloncurry's happiness, a sum of money would be placed to the credit of his (Piers') account in a certain Dublin Bank. In case of failure, the operation was, of course, to be reversed. . . .'

74

" On the 19th of February, 1807, the celebrated trial, Cloncurry v. Piers, for crim. con., commenced in the Court of King's Bench before Lord Chief Justice Downes. Damages were laid at £100,000. The case created great interest and resulted in a verdict for the plaintiff, £20,000 and costs. John Philpot Curran and Charles Kendal Bushe were the leading Counsel for Lord Cloncurry, and their speeches were what might be expected from such gifted advocates. Those who would wish to read the speeches should consult *Curran and His Contemporaries*, by Charles Philips. Piers put in no appearance at the trial. Haunted by the near approach of retribution, he packed his portmanteau and fled to the Isle of Man. By this proceeding his recognizances became, of course, forfeited to the Crown. After a time the strong arm of the law secured him; he gave what he could reluctantly enough, and his bond for the remainder. Assailed on all sides by creditors, Sir John Piers had a cottage built at Tristernagh, surrounded by a high wall, to protect himself from the minions of justice; but ruin and misfortune overtook him; his estates were sold out in the Encumbered Estates Court." (*Annals of Westmeath, Ancient and Modern*, by James Woods.)

I. *The Fête Champêtre*

Oh, gay lapped the waves on the shores of Lough Ennel
And sweet smelt the breeze 'mid the garlic and fennel,
But sweeter and gayer than either of these
Were the songs of the birds in Lord Belvedere's trees.

The light skiff is push'd from the weed-waving shore,
The rowlocks creak evenly under the oar,
And a boatload of beauty darts over the tide,
The Baron Cloncurry and also his bride.

Lord Belvedere sits like a priest in the prow,
'Tis the Lady Mount Cashel sits next to him now.
And both the de Blacquieres to balance the boat,
Was so much nobility ever afloat ?

The party's arranged on the opposite shore,
Lord Clonmore is present and one or two more,
But why has the Lady Cloncurry such fears ?
Oh, one of the guests will be Baronet Piers.

The grotto is reached and the parties alight,
The feast is spread out, and begob ! what a sight,
Pagodas of jelly in bowls of champagne,
And a tower of blancmange from the Baron Kilmaine.

In the shell-covered shelter the grotto affords
The meats and the pies are arranged on the boards,
The nobility laugh and are free from all worry
Excepting the bride of the Baron Cloncurry.

But his lordship is gayer than ever before,
He laughs like the ripples that lap the lake shore,
Nor thinks that his bride has the slightest of fears
Lest one of the guests be the Baronet Piers.

A curricle rolling along on the grass,
The servants make way to allow it to pass,
A high-stepping grey and the wheels flashing yellow
And Sir John in the seat, what a capital fellow !

Huzza for Sir John ! and huzza for the fête,
For without his assistance no fête is complete;
Oh, gay is the garland the ladies will wreathe
For the handsomest blade in the County Westmeath.

77

The harness is off with a jingle of steel,
The grey in the grass crops an emerald meal,
Sir John saunters up with a smile and a bow
And the Lady Cloncurry is next to him now.

Her eyes on the landscape, she don't seem to hear
The passing remark he designs for her ear,
For smooth as a phantom and proud as a stork
The Lady Cloncurry continues her walk.

II. The Attempt

I love your brown curls, | black in rain, my colleen,
  I love your grey eyes, | by this verdant shore
Two Derravaraghs | to plunge into and drown me,
  Hold not those lakes of | light so near me more.

My hand lies yellow | and hairy in your pink hand,
  Fragilis rubra | of the bramble flower,
Yet soft and thornless, | cool and as caressing
  As grasses bending | heavy with a shower.

See how the clouds twist | over in the twilight,
  See how the gale is | ruffling up the lake;
Lie still for ever | on this little peninsula,
  Heart beat and heart beat | steady till we wake.

Hear how the beech trees | roar above Glencara,
  See how the fungus | circles in the shade,
Roar trees and moan, you | gliding royal daughters,
  Circle us with poison, | we are not afraid.

Gothic on Gothic | my abbey soars around me,
  I've walks and avenues | emerald from rain,
Plentiful timber | in a lake reflected,
  And creamy meadowsweet | scenting my demesne.

Press to your cheeks | my hand so hot and wasted,
  Smooth with my fingers | the freckles of your frown,
Take you my abbey, | it is yours for always,
  I am so full of | love that I shall drown.

> *I lie by the lake water*
> *And you, Cloncurry, not near,*
> *I live in a girl's answer,*
> *You, in a bawd's fear.*

III.   The Exile

On Mannin's rough coast-line the twilight descending
  With its last dying rays on thy height, O Snaefell!
A refuge of dark to the Island is lending
  And to yon *cottage ornée* that lies in the dell.

Its helpless inhabitant dare not appear in
  The rain-weathered streets of adjacent Rumsaa,
But he sees in his dreams the green island of Erin
  And he sits in an orat'ry most of the day.

Yet sometimes, at night, when the waves in commotion
  Are tumbling about round the long point of Ayr,
He strides through the tamarisks down to the ocean
  Beyond the lush curraghs of sylvan Lezayre.

Alone with his thoughts when the wild waves are beating
  He walks round to Jurby along the wet sand,
And there, where the moon shows the waves are retreating,
  He too would retreat to his own native land.

O.P.—H

IV. The Return

My speculated avenues are wasted,
   The artificial lake is choked and dry,
My old delight by other lips is tasted,
   Now I can only build my walls and die.

I'll nail the southern wall with Irish peaches,
   Portloman cuttings warmed in silver suns,
And eastwards to Lough Iron's reedy reaches
   I'll build against the vista and the duns.

To westward where the avenue approaches
   Since they have felled the trees of my demesne,
And since I'll not be visited by coaches,
   I'll build a mighty wall against the rain.

And from the North, lest you, Malone, should spy me,
   You, Sunderlin of Baronstown, the peer,
I'll fill your eye with all the stone that's by me
   And live four-square protected in my fear.

Blue dragonflies dart on and do not settle,
    Live things stay not; although my walls are high,
They keep not out the knapweed and the nettle,
    Stone are my coffin walls, waiting till I die.

V. Tristernagh To-day

In the ivy dusty is the old lock rusty
    That opens rasping on the place of graves,
'Tis no home for mortals behind those portals
    Where the shining dock grows and the nettle waves.
Of the walls so ferny, near Tristernagh churchyard,
    Often the learned historians write,
And the Abbey splendificent, most magnificent,
    Ribbed and springing in ancient night.

Kyrie eleison ! blessed St. Bison !
    Holy Piran !   Veronica's Veil !
SS. Columb, Colman and St. Attracta,
    Likewise St. Hector, please aid my tale !
Holy Virgin !   What's that emergin' ?
    I daren't go down in the place of graves,
Head of a dragonfly, twenty times magnified,
    Creeping diagonal, out of the caves !

Dockleaves lapping it, maidenhair flapping it,

   Blue veins mapping it, skin of the moon,

Suck of the bog in it, cold of the frog in it,

   Keep it away from me, shrouded cocoon.

The worms are moving this soft and smooth thing

   And I'm the creature for foolish fears,

There's not a feature that's super nature

   'Tis only rational, 'tis

SIR

JOHN

PIERS.

Myfanwy

Kind o'er the *kinderbank* leans my Myfanwy,
  White o'er the play-pen the sheen of her dress,
Fresh from the bathroom and soft in the nursery
  Soap-scented fingers I long to caress.

Were you a prefect and head of your dormit'ry ?
  Were you a hockey girl, tennis or gym ?
Who was your favourite ?   Who had a crush on you ?
  Which were the baths where they taught you to swim ?

Smooth down the Avenue glitters the bicycle,
  Black-stockinged legs under navy-blue serge,
Home and Colonial, Star, International,
  Balancing bicycle leant on the verge.

Trace me your wheel-tracks, you fortunate bicycle,
  Out of the shopping and into the dark,
Back down the Avenue, back to the pottingshed,
  Back to the house on the fringe of the park.

Golden the light on the locks of Myfanwy,
  Golden the light on the book on her knee,
Finger-marked pages of Rackham's Hans Andersen,
  Time for the children to come down to tea.

Oh ! Fuller's angel-cake, Robertson's marmalade,
  Liberty lampshade, come, shine on us all,
My ! what a spread for the friends of Myfanwy
  Some in the alcove and some in the hall.

Then what sardines in the half-lighted passages !
  Locking of fingers in long hide-and-seek.
You will protect me, my silken Myfanwy,
  Ringleader, tom-boy, and chum to the weak.

Myfanwy at Oxford

Pink may, double may, dead laburnum
   Shedding an Anglo-Jackson shade,
Shall we ever, my staunch Myfanwy,
   Bicycle down to North Parade ?
Kant on the handle-bars, Marx in the saddlebag,
   Light my touch on your shoulder-blade.

Sancta Hilda, Myfanwyatia
   Evansensis—I hold your heart,
Willowy banks of a willowy Cherwell a
   Willowy figure with lips apart,
Strong and willowy, strong to pillow me,
   Gold Myfanwy, kisses and art.

Tubular bells of tall St. Barnabas,
   Single clatter above St. Paul,
Chasuble, acolyte, incense-offering,
   Spectacled faces held in thrall.
There in the nimbus and Comper tracery
   Gold Myfanwy blesses us all.

Gleam of gas upon Oxford station,
  Gleam of gas on her straight gold hair,
Hair flung back with an ostentation,
  Waiting alone for a girl friend there.
Second in Mods and a Third in Theology
  Come to breathe again Oxford air.

Her Myfanwy as in Cadena days,
  Her Myfanwy, a schoolgirl voice,
Tentative brush of a cheek in a cocoa crush,
  Coffee and Ulysses, Tennyson, Joyce,
Alpha-minded and other dimensional,
  Freud or Calvary ?   Take your choice.

Her Myfanwy ?   *My* Myfanwy.
  Bicycle bells in a Boar's Hill Pine,
Stedman Triple from All Saints' steeple,
  Tom and his hundred and one at nine,
Bells of Butterfield, caught in Keble,
  Sally and backstroke answer *"Mine !"*

Lake District

" On their way back they found the girls at Ease-
dale, sitting beside the cottage where they sell
ginger beer in August." (*Peer and Heiress*, Walter
Besant.)

I pass the cruet and I see the lake

   Running with light, beyond the garden pine,

    That lake whose waters make me dream her mine.

Up to the top board mounting for my sake,

For me she breathes, for me each soft intake,

    For me the plunge, the lake and limbs combine.

    I pledge her in non-alcoholic wine

And give the H.P. Sauce another shake.

Spirit of Grasmere, bells of Ambleside,

   Sing you and ring you, water bells, for me;

    You water-colour waterfalls may froth.

Long hiking holidays will yet provide

   Long stony lanes and back at six to tea

    And Heinz's ketchup on the tablecloth.

In Westminster Abbey

Let me take this other glove off
    As the *vox humana* swells,
And the beauteous fields of Eden
    Bask beneath the Abbey bells.
Here, where England's statesmen lie,
Listen to a lady's cry.

Gracious Lord, oh bomb the Germans.
    Spare their women for Thy Sake,
And if that is not too easy
    We will pardon Thy Mistake.
But, gracious Lord, whate'er shall be,
Don't let anyone bomb me.

Keep our Empire undismembered
    Guide our Forces by Thy Hand,
Gallant blacks from far Jamaica,
    Honduras and Togoland;
Protect them Lord in all their fights,
And, even more, protect the whites.

Think of what our Nation stands for,
Books from Boots' and country lanes,
Free speech, free passes, class distinction,
Democracy and proper drains.
Lord, put beneath Thy special care
One-eighty-nine Cadogan Square.

Although dear Lord I am a sinner,
I have done no major crime;
Now I'll come to Evening Service
Whensoever I have the time.
So, Lord, reserve for me a crown,
And do not let my shares go down.

I will labour for Thy Kingdom,
Help our lads to win the war,
Send white feathers to the cowards
Join the Women's Army Corps,
Then wash the Steps around Thy Throne
In the Eternal Safety Zone.

Now I feel a little better,
What a treat to hear Thy Word,
Where the bones of leading statesmen,
Have so often been interr'd.
And now, dear Lord, I cannot wait
Because I have a luncheon date.

Senex

Oh would I could subdue the flesh
   Which sadly troubles me !
And then perhaps could view the flesh
As though I never knew the flesh
   And merry misery.

To see the golden hiking girl
   With wind about her hair,
The tennis-playing, biking girl,
The wholly-to-my-liking girl,
   To see and not to care.

At sundown on my tricycle
   I tour the Borough's edge,
And icy as an icicle
See bicycle by bicycle
   Stacked waiting in the hedge.

Get down from me !   I thunder there,
   You spaniels !   Shut your jaws !

Your teeth are stuffed with underwear,
Suspenders torn asunder there
    And buttocks in your paws !

Oh whip the dogs away my Lord,
    They make me ill with lust.
Bend bare knees down to pray, my lord,
Teach sulky lips to say, my Lord,
    That flaxen hair is dust.

Olney Hymns

Oh God the Olney Hymns abound
    With words of Grace which Thou didst choose,
And wet the elm above the hedge
    Reflected in the winding Ouse.

Pour in my soul unemptied floods
    That stand between the slopes of clay,
Till deep beyond a deeper depth
    This Olney day is any day.

On a Portrait of a Deaf Man

The kind old face, the egg-shaped head,
  The tie, discreetly loud,
The loosely fitting shooting clothes,
  A closely fitting shroud.

He liked old City dining-rooms,
  Potatoes in their skin,
But now his mouth is wide to let
  The London clay come in.

He took me on long silent walks
  In country lanes when young,
He knew the name of ev'ry bird
  But not the song it sung.

And when he could not hear me speak
  He smiled and looked so wise
That now I do not like to think
  Of maggots in his eyes.

He liked the rain-washed Cornish air
　　And smell of ploughed-up soil,
He liked a landscape big and bare
　　And painted it in oil.

But least of all he liked that place
　　Which hangs on Highgate Hill
Of soaked Carrara-covered earth
　　For Londoners to fill.

He would have liked to say good-bye,
　　Shake hands with many friends,
In Highgate now his finger-bones
　　Stick through his finger-ends.

You, God, who treat him thus and thus,
　　Say " Save his soul and pray."
You ask me to believe You and
　　I only see decay.

Saint Cadoc

A flame of rushlight in the cell
On holy walls and holy well
And to the west the thundering bay
With soaking seaweed, sand and spray,
    Oh good St. Cadoc pray for me
    Here in your cell beside the sea.

Somewhere the tree, the yellowing oak,
Is waiting for the woodman's stroke,
Waits for the chisel saw and plane
To prime it for the earth again
    And in the earth, for me inside,
    The generous oak tree will have died.

St. Cadoc blest the woods of ash
Bent landwards by the Western lash,
He loved the veinéd threshold stones
Where sun might sometime bleach his bones
    He had no cowering fear of death
    For breath of God was Cadoc's breath.

98

Some cavern generates the germs
To send my body to the worms,
To-day some red hands make the shell
To blow my soul away to Hell
  To-day a pair walks newly married
  Along the path where I'll be carried.

St. Cadoc, when the wind was high,
Saw angels in the Cornish sky
As ocean rollers curled and poured
Their loud Hosannas to the Lord,
  His little cell was not too small
  For that great Lord who made them all.

Here where St. Cadoc sheltered God
The archæologist has trod,
Yet death is now the gentle shore
With Land upon the cliffs before
  And in his cell beside the sea
  The Celtic saint has prayed for me.

Blackfriars

By the shot tower near the chimneys,
  Off the road to Waterloo,
Stands the cottage of " The Agéd "
  As in eighteen-forty-two.
Over brickwork, brownish brickwork,
  Lilac hangs in London sun
And by light fantastic clockwork
  Moves the drawbridge, sounds the gun.
When the sunset in the side streets
  Brought the breezes up the tide,
Floated bits of daily journals,
  Stable smells and silverside.
And the gaslight, yellow gaslight,
  Flaring in its wiry cage,
Like the Prison Scene in *Norval*
  On the old Olympic stage,
Lit the archway as the thunder,
  And the rumble and the roll,
Heralded a little handcart,
  And " The Agéd " selling coal.

Henley-on-Thames

I see the winding water make
A short and then a shorter lake
    As here stand I,
    And house-boat high
Survey the Upper Thames.
  By sun the mud is amber-dyed
  In ripples slow and flat and wide,
  That flap against the house-boat side
And flop away in gems.

In mud and elder-scented shade
A reach away the breach is made
    By dive and shout
    That circles out
To Henley tower and town;
  And " Boats for Hire " the rafters ring,
  And pink on white the roses cling,
  And red the bright geraniums swing
In baskets dangling down.

When shall I see the Thames again ?
The prow-promoted gems again,
    As beefy ATS
    Without their hats
Come shooting through the bridge ?
  And " cheerioh " and " cheeri-bye "
  Across the waste of waters die,
  And low the mists of evening lie
And lightly skims the midge.

Parliament Hill Fields

Rumbling under blackened girders, Midland, bound for
                                      Cricklewood,

Puffed its sulphur to the sunset where that Land of Laun-
                                      dries stood.

Rumble under, thunder over, train and tram alternate go,

Shake the floor and smudge the ledger, Charrington, Sells,
                                      Dale and Co.,

Nuts and nuggets in the window, trucks along the lines
                                      below.

When the Bon Marché was shuttered, when the feet were
                                      hot and tired,

Outside Charrington's we waited, by the " STOP HERE
                                      IF REQUIRED ",

Launched aboard the shopping basket, sat precipitately
                                      down,

Rocked past Zwanziger the baker's, and the terrace blackish
                                      brown,

And the curious Anglo-Norman parish church of Kentish
                                      Town.

Till the tram went over thirty, sighting terminus again,

Past municipal lawn tennis and the bobble-hanging plane;

Soft the light suburban evening caught our ashlar-speckled
spire,

Eighteen-sixty Early English, as the mighty elms retire

Either side of Brookfield Mansions flashing fine French-
window fire.

Oh the after-tram-ride quiet, when we heard a mile beyond,

Silver music from the bandstand, barking dogs by Highgate
Pond;

Up the hill where stucco houses in Virginia creeper drown—

And my childish wave of pity, seeing children carrying down

Sheaves of drooping dandelions to the courts of Kentish
Town.

A Subaltern's Love-song

Miss J. Hunter Dunn, Miss J. Hunter Dunn,
Furnish'd and burnish'd by Aldershot sun,
What strenuous singles we played after tea,
We in the tournament—you against me !

Love-thirty, love-forty, oh ! weakness of joy,
The speed of a swallow, the grace of a boy,
With carefullest carelessness, gaily you won,
I am weak from your loveliness, Joan Hunter Dunn.

Miss Joan Hunter Dunn, Miss Joan Hunter Dunn,
How mad I am, sad I am, glad that you won.
The warm-handled racket is back in its press,
But my shock-headed victor, she loves me no less.

Her father's euonymus shines as we walk,
And swing past the summer-house, buried in talk,
And cool the verandah that welcomes us in
To the six-o'clock news and a lime-juice and gin.

105

The scent of the conifers, sound of the bath,
The view from my bedroom of moss-dappled path,
As I struggle with double-end evening tie,
For we dance at the Golf Club, my victor and I.

On the floor of her bedroom lie blazer and shorts
And the cream-coloured walls are be-trophied with sports,
And westering, questioning settles the sun
On your low-leaded window, Miss Joan Hunter Dunn.

The Hillman is waiting, the light's in the hall,
The pictures of Egypt are bright on the wall,
My sweet, I am standing beside the oak stair
And there on the landing's the light on your hair.

By roads " not adopted ", by woodlanded ways,
She drove to the club in the late summer haze,
Into nine-o'clock Camberley, heavy with bells
And mushroomy, pine-woody, evergreen smells.

Miss Joan Hunter Dunn, Miss Joan Hunter Dunn,
I can hear from the car-park the dance has begun.
Oh ! full Surrey twilight ! importunate band !
Oh ! strongly adorable tennis-girl's hand !

Around us are Rovers and Austins afar,
Above us, the intimate roof of the car,
And here on my right is the girl of my choice,
With the tilt of her nose and the chime of her voice,

And the scent of her wrap, and the words never said,
And the ominous, ominous dancing ahead.
We sat in the car park till twenty to one
And now I'm engaged to Miss Joan Hunter Dunn.

Bristol

Green upon the flooded Avon shone the after-storm-wet-sky
Quick the struggling withy branches let the leaves of
autumn fly
And a star shone over Bristol, wonderfully far and high.

Ringers in an oil-lit belfry—Bitton ? Kelston ? who shall
say ?—
Smoothly practising a plain course, caverned out the dying
day
As their melancholy music flooded up and ebbed away.

Then all Somerset was round me and I saw the clippers ride,
High above the moonlit houses, triple-masted on the tide,
By the tall embattled church-towers of the Bristol waterside.

And an undersong to branches dripping into pools and wells
Out of multitudes of elm trees over leagues of hills and dells
Was the mathematic pattern of a plain course on the bells.*

```
*1  2  2  4  4  5  5  3  3  1  1
 2  1  4  2  5  4  3  5  1  3  2
 3  4  1  5  2  3  4  1  5  2  3
 4  3  5  1  3  2  1  4  2  5  4
 5  5  3  3  1  1  2  2  4  4  5
```

On an Old-Fashioned Water-Colour of Oxford

(Early Twentieth-Century Date)

Shines, billowing cold and gold from Cumnor Hurst,
    A winter sunset on wet cobbles, where
    By Canterbury Gate the fishtails flare.
Someone in Corpus reading for a first
Pulls down red blinds and flounders on, immers'd
    In Hegel, heedless of the yellow glare
    On porch and pinnacle and window square,
The brown stone crumbling where the skin has burst.

A late, last luncheon staggers out of Peck
    And hires a hansom: from half-flooded grass
    Returning athletes bark at what they see.
But we will mount the horse-tram's upper deck
    And wave salute to Buols', as we pass
    Bound for the Banbury Road in time for tea.

A Lincolnshire Tale

Kirkby with Muckby-cum-Sparrowby-cum-Spinx
Is down a long lane in the county of Lincs,
And often on Wednesdays, well-harnessed and spruce,
I would drive into Wiss over Winderby Sluice.

A whacking great sunset bathed level and drain
From Kirkby with Muckby to Beckby-on-Bain,
And I saw, as I journeyed, my marketing done
Old Caistorby tower take the last of the sun.

The night air grew nippy.   An autumn mist roll'd
(In a scent of dead cabbages) down from the wold,
In the ocean of silence that flooded me round
The crunch of the wheels was a comforting sound.

The lane lengthened narrowly into the night
With the Bain on its left bank, the drain on its right,
And feebly the carriage-lamps glimmered ahead
When all of a sudden *the pony fell dead.*

111

The remoteness was awful, the stillness intense,
Of invisible fenland, around and immense;
And out of the dark, with a roar and a swell,
Swung, hollowly thundering, Speckleby bell.

Though myself the Archdeacon for many a year,
I had not summoned courage for visiting here;
Our incumbents were mostly eccentric or sad
But—*the Speckleby Rector was said to be mad.*

Oh cold was the ev'ning and tall was the tower
And strangely compelling the tenor bell's power !
As loud on the reed-beds and strong through the dark
It toll'd from the church in the tenantless park.

The mansion was ruined, the empty demesne
Was slowly reverting to marshland again—
Marsh where the village was, grass in the Hall,
And the church and the Rectory waiting to fall.

And even in springtime with kingcups about
And stumps of old oak-trees attempting to sprout,
'Twas a sinister place, neither fenland nor wold,
And doubly forbidding in darkness and cold.

As down swung the tenor, a beacon of sound,
Over listening acres of waterlogged ground
I stood by the tombs to see pass and repass
The gleam of a taper, through clear leaded glass,

And such lighting of lights in the thunderous roar
That heart summoned courage to hand at the door;
I grated it open on scents I knew well,
The dry smell of damp rot, the hassocky smell.

What a forest of woodwork in ochres and grains
Unevenly doubled in diamonded panes,
And over the plaster, so textured with time,
Sweet discoloration of umber and lime.

The candles ensconced on each high pannelled pew
Brought the caverns of brass-studded baize into view,
But the roof and its rafters were lost to the sight
As they soared to the dark of the Lincolnshire night:

And high from the chancel arch paused to look down
A sign-painter's beasts in their fight for the Crown,
While massive, impressive, and still as the grave
A three-decker pulpit frowned over the nave.

Shall I ever forget what a stillness was there
When the bell ceased its tolling and thinned on the air ?
Then an opening door showed a long pair of bands
And the Rector himself in his gown and his bands.

*   *   *   *   *

Such a fell Visitation I shall not forget,
Such a rush through the dark, that I rush through it yet,
And I pray, as the bells ring o'er fenland and hill,
That the Speckleby acres be tenantless still.

St. Barnabas, Oxford

How long was the peril, how breathless the day,
In topaz and beryl, the sun dies away,
His rays lying static at quarter to six
On polychromatical lacing of bricks.
Good Lord, as the angelus floats down the road,
Byzantine St. Barnabas, be Thine Abode.

Where once the fritillaries hung in the grass
A baldachin pillar is guarding the Mass.
Farewell to blue meadows we loved not enough,
And elms in whose shadows were Glanville and Clough
Not poets but clergymen hastened to meet
Thy redden'd remorselessness, Cardigan Street.

An Archæological Picnic

In this high pasturage, this Blunden time,
    With Lady's Finger, Smokewort, Lovers' Loss,
And lin-lan-lone a Tennysonian chime
    Stirring the sorrel and the gold-starred moss,
    Cool is the chancel, bright the altar cross.

Drink, Mary, drink your fizzy lemonade
    And leave the king-cups; take your grey felt hat;
Here, where the low-side window lends a shade,
    There, where the key lies underneath the mat,
    The rude forefathers of the hamlet sat.

Sweet smell of cerements and of cold wet stones,
    Hassock and cassock, paraffin and pew;
Green in a light which that sublime Burne-Jones
    White-hot and wondering from the glass-kiln drew,
    Gleams and re-gleams this Trans arcade anew.

So stand you waiting, freckled innocence !
    For me the squinch and squint and Trans arcade;
For you, where meadow grass is evidence,
    With flattened pattern, of our picnic made,
    One bottle more of fizzy lemonade.

May-Day Song for North Oxford

(Annie Laurie Tune)

Belbroughton Road is bonny, and pinkly bursts the spray
Of prunus and forsythia across the public way,
For a full spring-tide of blossom seethed and departed hence,
Leaving land-locked pools of jonquils by sunny garden fence.

And a constant sound of flushing runneth from windows
where
The toothbrush too is airing in this new North Oxford air
From Summerfields to Lynam's, the thirsty tarmac dries,
And a Cherwell mist dissolveth on elm-discovering skies.

Oh ! well-bound Wells and Bridges !   Oh ! earnest ethical
search
For the wide high-table λογος of St. C. S. Lewis's Church.
This diamond-eyed Spring morning my soul soars up the
slope
Of a right good rough-cast buttress on the housewall of my
hope.

118

And open-necked and freckled, where once there grazed the
cows,

Emancipated children swing on old apple boughs,

And pastel-shaded book rooms bring New Ideas to birth

As the whitening hawthorn only hears the heart beat of the
earth.

Before Invasion, 1940

Still heavy with may, and the sky ready to fall,
Meadows buttercup high, shed and chicken and wire ?
And here where the wind leans on a sycamore silver wall,
Are you still taller than sycamores, gallant Victorian spire ?

Still, fairly intact, and demolishing squads about,
Bracketed station lamp with your oil-light taken away ?
Weep flowering currant, while your bitter cascades are out,
Born in an age of railways, for flowering into to-day !

Ireland with Emily

Bells are booming down the bohreens,
  White the mist along the grass.
Now the Julias, Maeves and Maureens
  Move between the fields to Mass.
Twisted trees of small green apple
Guard the decent whitewashed chapel,
Gilded gates and doorway grained
Pointed windows richly stained
  With many-coloured Munich glass.

See the black-shawled congregations
  On the broidered vestment gaze
Murmur past the painted stations
  As Thy Sacred Heart displays
Lush Kildare of scented meadows,
Roscommon, thin in ash-tree shadows,
And Westmeath the lake-reflected,
Spreading Leix the hill-protected,
  Kneeling all in silver haze ?

In yews and woodbine, walls and guelder,
  Nettle-deep the faithful rest,
Winding leagues of flowering elder,
  Sycamore with ivy dressed,
Ruins in demesnes deserted,
Bog-surrounded bramble-skirted—
Townlands rich or townlands mean as
These, oh, counties of them screen us
  In the Kingdom of the West.

Stony seaboard, far and foreign,
  Stony hills poured over space,
Stony outcrop of the Burren,
  Stones in every fertile place,
Little fields with boulders dotted,
Grey-stone shoulders saffron-spotted,
Stone-walled cabins thatched with reeds,
Where a Stone Age people breeds
  The last of Europe's stone age race.

Has it held, the warm June weather ?
  Draining shallow sea-pools dry,
When we bicycled together
  Down the bohreens fuchsia-high.

Till there rose, abrupt and lonely,
A ruined abbey, chancel only,
Lichen-crusted, time-befriended,
Soared the arches, splayed and splendid,
  Romanesque against the sky.

There in pinnacled protection,
  One extinguished family waits
A Church of Ireland resurrection
  By the broken, rusty gates.
Sheepswool, straw and droppings cover,
Graves of spinster, rake and lover,
Whose fantastic mausoleum
Sings its own seablown Te Deum,
  In and out the slipping slates.

Margate, 1940

From out the Queen's Highcliffe for weeks at a stretch
I watched how the mower evaded the vetch,
So that over the putting-course rashes were seen
Of pink and of yellow among the burnt green.

How restful to putt, when the strains of a band
Announced a *thé dansant* was on at the Grand,
While over the privet, comminglingly clear,
I heard lesser " Co-Optimists " down by the pier.

How lightly municipal, meltingly tarr'd,
Were the walks through the Laws by the Queen's Promenade
As soft over Cliftonville languished the light
Down Harold Road, Norfolk Road, into the night.

Oh ! then what a pleasure to see the ground floor
With tables for two laid as tables for four,

124

And bottles of sauce and Kia-Ora[1] and squash
Awaiting their owners who'd gone up to wash—

Who had gone up to wash the ozone from their skins
The sand from their legs and the Rock from their chins,
To prepare for an evening of dancing and cards
And forget the sea-breeze on the dry promenades.

From third floor and fourth floor the children looked down
Upon ribbons of light in the salt-scented town;
And drowning the trams roared the sound of the sea
As it washed in the shingle the scraps of their tea.

*   *   *   *   *

Beside the Queen's Highcliffe now rank grows the vetch,
Now dark is the terrace, a storm-battered stretch;
And I think, as the fairy-lit sights I recall,
It is those we are fighting for, foremost of all.

[1] Pronounced " Kee-ora ".

Invasion Exercise on the Poultry Farm

Softly croons the radiogram, loudly hoot the owls,
Judy gives the door a slam and goes to feed the fowls.
Marty rolls a Craven A around her ruby lips
And runs her yellow fingers down her corduroyed hips,
Shuts her mouth and screws her eyes and puffs her fag alight
And hears some most peculiar cries that echo through the
night.

Ting-a-ling the telephone, to-whit to-whoo the owls,
Judy, Judy, Judy girl, and have you fed the fowls ?
No answer as the poultry gate is swinging there ajar.
Boom the bombers overhead, between the clouds a star,
And just outside, among the arks, in a shadowy sheltered
place
Lie Judy and a paratroop in horrible embrace.
Ting-a-ling the telephone.   " Yes, this is Marty Hayne."
" Have you seen a paratroop come walking down your lane ?
He may be on your premises, he may be somewhere near,
And if he is report the fact to Major Maxton-Weir."
Marty moves in dread towards the window—standing there

Draws the curtain—sees the guilty movement of the pair.[1]

White with rage and lined with age but strong and sturdy
    still

Marty now co-ordinates her passions and her will,

She will teach that Judy girl to trifle with the heart

And go and kiss a paratroop like any common tart.

She switches up the radiogram and covered by the blare

She goes and gets a riding whip and whirls it in the air,

She fetches down a length of rope and rushes, breathing hard

To let the couple have it for embracing in the yard.

Crack ! the pair are paralysed.   Click ! they cannot stir.

Zip ! she's trussed the paratroop.   There's no embracing *her*.

" Hullo, hullo, hullo, hullo . . . Major Maxton-Weir ?

I've trussed your missing paratroop.   He's waiting for you
    here.''

[1] These lines in italic are by Henry Oscar.

127

The Planster's Vision

Cut down that timber ! Bells, too many and strong,
   Pouring their music through the branches bare,
   From moon-white church-towers down the windy **air**
Have pealed the centuries out with Evensong.
Remove those cottages, a huddled throng !
   Too many babies have been born in there,
   Too many coffins, bumping down the stair,
Carried the old their garden paths along.

I have a Vision of The Future, chum,
   The workers' flats in fields of soya beans
     Tower up like silver pencils, score on score:
And Surging Millions hear the Challenge come
   From microphones in communal canteens
     " No Right ! No Wrong ! All's perfect, evermore."

In a Bath Teashop

" Let us not speak, for the love we bear one another—
    Let us hold hands and look."
She, such a very ordinary little woman;
    He, such a thumping crook;
But both, for a moment, little lower than the angels
    In the teashop's ingle-nook.

Before the Anæsthetic,
or
A Real Fright

Intolerably sad, profound
St. Giles's bells are ringing round,
They bring the slanting summer rain
To tap the chestnut boughs again
Whose shadowy cave of rainy leaves
The gusty belfry-song receives.
Intolerably sad and true,
Victorian red and jewel* blue,
The mellow bells are ringing round
And charge the evening light with sound,
And I look motionless from bed
On heavy trees and purple red
And hear the midland bricks and tiles
Throw back the bells of stone St. Giles,
Bells, ancient now as castle walls,
Now hard and new as pitchpine stalls,

* Adjective from Rumer Godden.

Now full with help from ages past,
Now dull with death and hell at last.
Swing up ! and give me hope of life,
Swing down ! and plunge the surgeon's knife.
I, breathing for a moment, see
Death wing himself away from me
And think, as on this bed I lie,
Is it extinction when I die ?
I move my limbs and use my sight ;
Not yet, thank God, not yet the Night.
Oh better far those echoing hells
Half-threaten'd in the pealing bells
Than that this " I " should cease to be—
Come quickly, Lord, come quick to me.
St. Giles's bells are asking now
" And hast thou known the Lord, hast thou ? "
St. Giles's bells, they richly ring
" And was that Lord our Christ the King ? "
St. Giles's bells they hear me call
I never knew the Lord at all.
Oh not in me your Saviour dwells
You ancient, rich St. Giles's bells.
Illuminated missals—spires—
Wide screens and decorated quires—

131

All these I loved, and on my knees
I thanked myself for knowing these
And watched the morning sunlight pass
Through richly stained Victorian glass
And in the colour-shafted air
I, kneeling, thought the Lord was there.
Now, lying in the gathering mist
I know that Lord did not exist;
Now, lest this " I " should cease to be,
Come, real Lord, come quick to me.
With every gust the chestnut sighs,
With every breath, a mortal dies;
The man who smiled alone, alone,
And went his journey on his own
With " Will you give my wife this letter,
In case, of course, I don't get better ? "
Waits for his coffin lid to close
On waxen head and yellow toes.
Almighty Saviour, had I Faith
There'd be no fight with kindly Death.
Intolerably long and deep
St. Giles's bells swing on in sleep:
" But still you go from here alone "
Say all the bells about the Throne.

On Hearing the Full Peal of Ten Bells from Christ Church, Swindon, Wilts.

Your peal of ten ring over then this town,
Ring on my men nor ever ring them down.
This winter chill, let sunset spill cold fire
On villa'd hill and on Sir Gilbert's spire,
So new, so high, so pure, so broach'd, so tall.
Long run the thunder of the bells through all !

Oh still white headstones on these fields of sound
Hear you the wedding joybells wheeling round ?
Oh brick-built breeding boxes of new souls,
Hear how the pealing through the louvres rolls !
Now birth and death-reminding bells ring clear,
Loud under 'planes and over changing gear.

133

Youth and Age on Beaulieu River, Hants

Early sun on Beaulieu water
Lights the undersides of oaks,
Clumps of leaves it floods and blanches,
All transparent glow the branches
Which the double sunlight soaks;
To her craft on Beaulieu water
Clemency the General's daughter
Pulls across with even strokes.

Schoolboy-sure she is this morning;
Soon her sharpie's rigg'd and free.
Cool beneath a garden awning
Mrs. Fairclough, sipping tea
And raising large long-distance glasses
As the little sharpie passes,
Sighs our sailor girl to see:

Tulip figure, so appealing,
Oval face, so serious-eyed,

Tree-roots pass'd and muddy beaches.
On to huge and lake-like reaches,
       Soft and sun-warm, see her glide—
    Slacks the slim young limbs revealing,
    Sun-brown arm the tiller feeling—
       With the wind and with the tide.

    Evening light will bring the water,
       Day-long sun will burst the bud,
    Clemency, the General's daughter,
       Will return upon the flood.
But the older woman only
Knows the ebb-tide leaves her lonely
       With the shining fields of mud.

East Anglian Bathe

Oh when the early morning at the seaside
    Took us with hurrying steps from Horsey Mere
To see the whistling bent-grass on the leeside
    And then the tumbled breaker-line appear,
On high, the clouds with mighty adumbration
    Sailed over us to seaward fast and clear
And jellyfish in quivering isolation
    Lay silted in the dry sand of the breeze
And we, along the table-land of beach blown
    Went gooseflesh from our shoulders to our knees
And ran to catch the football, each to each thrown,
    In the soft and swirling music of the seas.

There splashed about our ankles as we waded
    Those intersecting wavelets morning-cold,
And sudden dark a patch of sea was shaded,
    And sudden light, another patch would hold
The warmth of whirling atoms in a sun-shot

And underwater sandstorm green and gold.
So in we dived and louder than a gunshot
    Sea-water broke in fountains down the ear.
How cold the bathe, how chattering cold the drying,
    How welcoming the inland reeds appear,
The wood-smoke and the breakfast and the frying,
    And your warm freshwater ripples, Horsey Mere.

Sunday Afternoon Service in
St. Enodoc Church, Cornwall

Come on ! come on !   This hillock hides the spire,
Now that one and now none.   As winds about
The burnished path through lady's finger, thyme
And bright varieties of saxifrage,
So grows the tinny tenor faint or loud
And all things draw towards St. Enodoc.

Come on ! come on ! and it is five to three.

Paths, unfamiliar to golfers' brogues,
Cross the eleventh fairway broadside on
And leave the fourteenth tee for thirteenth green,
Ignoring Royal and Ancient, bound for God.
    Come on ! come on ! no longer bare of foot,
The sole grows hot in London shoes again.
Jack Lambourne in his Sunday navy-blue
Wears tie and collar, all from Selfridge's.
There's Enid with a silly parasol,
And Graham in gray flannel with a crease

138

Across the middle of his coat which lay
Pressed 'neath the box of his Meccano set,
Sunday to Sunday.

        Still, Come on! come on!
The tinny tenor.   Hover-flies remain
More than a moment on a ragwort bunch,
And people's passing shadows don't disturb
Red Admirals basking with their wings apart.

  A mile of sunny, empty sand away,
A mile of shallow pools and lugworm casts,
Safe, faint and surfy, laps the lowest tide.

  Even the villas have a Sunday look.
The Ransom mower's locked into the shed.
" I have a splitting headache from the sun,"
And bedroom windows flutter cheerful chintz
Where, double-aspirined, a mother sleeps;
While father in the loggia reads a book,
Large, desultory, birthday-present size,
Published with coloured plates by *Country Life,*
A Bernard Darwin on *The English Links*
Or Braid and Taylor on *The Mashie Shot.*
Come on ! come on! he thinks of Monday's round—
Come on ! come on ! that interlocking grip !
Come on ! come on ! he drops into a doze—

Come on! come on! more far and far away
The children climb a final stile to church;
Electoral Roll still flapping in the porch—
Then the cool silence of St. Enodoc.

My eyes, recovering in the sudden shade,
Discern the long-known little things within—
A map of France in damp above my pew,
Grey-blue of granite in the small arcade
(Late Perp: and not a Parker specimen
But roughly hewn on windy Bodmin Moor),
The modest windows palely glazed with green,
The smooth slate floor, the rounded wooden roof,
The Norman arch, the cable-moulded font—
All have a humble and West Country look.
Oh " drastic restoration " of the guide!
Oh three-light window by a Plymouth firm!
Absurd, truncated screen! oh sticky pews!
Embroidered altar-cloth! untended lamps!
So soaked in worship you are loved too well
For that dispassionate and critic stare
That I would use beyond the parish bounds
Biking in high-banked lanes from tower to tower
On sunny, antiquarian afternoons.

Come on ! come on ! a final pull.   Tom Blake
Stalks over from the bell-rope to his pew
Just as he slopes about the windy cliffs
Looking for wreckage in a likely tide,
Nor gives the Holy Table glance or nod.
A rattle as red baize is drawn aside,
Miss Rhoda Poulden pulls the tremolo,
The oboe, flute and vox humana stops;
A Village Voluntary fills the air
And ceases suddenly as it began,
Save for one oboe faintly humming on,
As slow the weary clergyman subsides
Tired with his bike-ride from the parish church.
He runs his hands once, twice, across his face
" Dearly beloved . . ." and a bumble-bee
Zooms itself free into the churchyard sun
And so my thoughts this happy Sabbathtide.
    Where deep cliffs loom enormous, where cascade
Mesembryanthemum and stone-crop down,
Where the gull looks no larger than a lark
Hung midway twixt the cliff-top and the sand,
Sun-shadowed valleys roll along the sea.
Forced by the backwash, see the nearest wave
Rise to a wall of huge, translucent green

141

And crumble into spray along the top
Blown seaward by the land-breeze.   Now she breaks
And in an arch of thunder plunges down
To burst and tumble, foam on top of foam,
Criss-crossing, baffled, sucked and shot again,
A waterfall of whiteness, down a rock,
Without a source but roller's furthest reach :
And tufts of sea-pink, high and dry for years,
Are flooded out of ledges, boulders seem
No bigger than a pebble washed about
In this tremendous tide.   Oh kindly slate !
To give me shelter in this crevice dry.
These shivering stalks of bent-grass, lucky plant,
Have better chance than I to last the storm.
Oh kindly slate of these unaltered cliffs,
Firm, barren substrate of our windy fields !
Oh lichened slate in walls, they knew your worth
Who raised you up to make this House of God
What faith was his, that dim, that Cornish saint,
Small rushlight of a long-forgotten church,
Who lived with God on this unfriendly shore,
Who knew He made the Atlantic and the stones
And destined seamen here to end their lives
Dashed on a rock, rolled over in the surf,

And not one hair forgotten.   Now they lie
In centuries of sand beside the church.
Less pitiable are they than the corpse
Of a large golfer, only four weeks dead,
This sunlit and sea-distant afternoon.
" Praise ye the Lord ! " and in another key
The Lord's name by harmonium be praised.
" The Second Evening and the Fourteenth Psalm."

The Irish Unionist's Farewell to Greta Hellstrom in 1922

Golden haired and golden hearted
  I would ever have you be,
As you were when last we parted
  Smiling slow and sad at me.
Oh ! the fighting down of passion !
  Oh ! the century-seeming pain—
Parting in this off-hand fashion
  In Dungarvan in the rain.

Slanting eyes of blue, unweeping,
  Stands my Swedish beauty where
Gusts of Irish rain are sweeping
  Round the statue in the square;
Corner boys against the walling
  Watch us furtively in vain,
And the Angelus is calling
  Through Dungarvan in the rain.

Gales along the Commeragh Mountains,
  Beating sleet on creaking signs,

144

Iron gutters turned to fountains,
    And the windscreen laced with lines,
And the evening getting later,
    And the ache—increased again,
As the distance grows the greater
    From Dungarvan in the rain.

There is no one now to wonder
    What eccentric sits in state
While the beech trees rock and thunder
    Round his gate-lodge and his gate.
Gone—the ornamental plaster,
    Gone—the overgrown demesne
And the car goes fast, and faster,
    From Dungarvan in the rain.

Had I kissed and drawn you to me,
    Had you yielded warm for cold,
What a power had pounded through me
    As I stroked your streaming gold !
You were right to keep us parted:
    Bound and parted we remain,
Aching, if unbroken hearted—
    Oh !   Dungarvan in the rain !

In Memory of Basil, Marquess of Dufferin and Ava

On such a morning as this
   with the birds ricocheting their music
Out of the whelming elms
   to a copper beech's embrace
And a sifting sound of leaves
   from multitudinous branches
Running across the park
   to a chequer of light on the lake,
On such a morning as this
   with *The Times* for June the eleventh
Left with coffee and toast
   you opened the breakfast-room window
And, sprawled on the southward terrace,
   Said: " That means war in September."

Friend of my youth, you are dead !
   and the long peal pours from the steeple
Over this sunlit quad
   in our University city

146

And soaks in Headington stone.
  Motionless stand the pinnacles.
Under a flying sky
  as though they too listened and waited
Like me for your dear return
  with a Bullingdon noise of an evening
In a Sports-Bugatti from Thame
  that belonged to a man in Magdalen.
Friend of my youth, you are dead !
  and the quads are empty without you.

Then there were people about.
  Each hour, like an Oxford archway,
Opened on long green lawns
  and distant unvisited buildings
And you my friend were explorer
  and so you remained to me always
Humorous, reckless, loyal—
  my kind, heavy-lidded companion.
Stop, oh many bells, stop
  pouring on roses and creeper
Your unremembering peal
  this hollow, unhallowed V.E. day,—
I am deaf to your notes and dead
  by a soldier's body in Burma.

South London Sketch, 1944

From Bermondsey to Wandsworth
  So many churches are,
Some with apsidal chancels,
  Some Perpendicular
And schools by E. R. Robson
  In the style of Norman Shaw
Where blue-serged adolescence learn'd
  To model and to draw.

Oh, in among the houses,
  The viaduct below,
Stood the Coffee Essence Factory
  Of Robinson and Co.
Burnt and brown and tumbled down
  And done with years ago
Where the waters of the Wandle do
  Lugubriously flow.

From dust of dead explosions,
    From scarlet-hearted fires,
All unconcerned this train draws in
    And smoothly that retires
And calmly rise on smoky skies
    Of intersected wires
The Nonconformist spirelets
    And the Church of England spires.

South London Sketch, 1844

Lavender Sweep is drowned in Wandsworth,
   Drowned in jessamine up to the neck,
Beetles sway upon bending grass leagues
   Shoulder-level to Tooting Bec.
Rich as Middlesex, rich in signboards,
   Lie the lover-trod lanes between,
Red Man, Green Man, Horse and Waggoner,
   Elms and sycamores round a green.
Burst, good June, with a rush this morning,
   Bindweed weave me an emerald rope
Sun, shine bright on the blossoming trellises,
   June and lavender, bring me hope.

Indoor Games near Newbury

In among the silver birches winding ways of tarmac wander

And the signs to Bussock Bottom, Tussock Wood and
Windy Brake,

Gabled lodges, tile-hung churches, catch the lights of our
Lagonda

As we drive to Wendy's party, lemon curd and Christmas
cake.

 Rich the makes of motor whirring,

 Past the pine-plantation purring

  Come up, Hupmobile, Delage !

 Short the way your chauffeurs travel,

 Crunching over private gravel

  Each from out his warm garáge.

Oh but Wendy, when the carpet yielded to my indoor pumps

 There you stood, your gold hair streaming,

 Handsome in the hall-light gleaming

There you looked and there you led me off into the game of
clumps

 Then the new Victrola playing

 And your funny uncle saying

151

" Choose your partners for a fox-trot ! Dance until its *tea*
o'clock !

" Come on, young 'uns, foot it featly ! "

Was it chance that paired us neatly,

I, who loved you so completely,

You, who pressed me closely to you, hard against your party
frock ?

" Meet me when you've finished eating ! " So we met and
no one found us.

Oh that dark and furry cupboard while the rest played
hide and seek !

Holding hands our two hearts beating in the bedroom silence
round us,

Holding hands and hardly hearing sudden footstep, thud
and shriek.

Love that lay too deep for kissing—

" Where *is* Wendy ? Wendy's missing ! "

Love so pure it *had* to end,

Love so strong that I was frighten'd

When you gripped my fingers tight and

Hugging, whispered " I'm your friend."

Good-bye Wendy ! Send the fairies, pinewood elf and larch
tree gnome,

Spingle-spangled stars are peeping

At the lush Lagonda creeping

Down the winding ways of tarmac to the leaded lights of
home.

    There, among the silver birches,

    All the bells of all the churches

Sounded in the bath-waste running out into the frosty air.

    Wendy speeded my undressing,

    Wendy is the sheet's caressing

    Wendy bending gives a blessing,

Holds me as I drift to dreamland, safe inside my slumber-
wear.

St. Saviour's, Aberdeen Park, Highbury, London, N.

With oh such peculiar branching and over-reaching of wire
  Trolley-bus standards pick their threads from the London
                                           sky
Diminishing up the perspective, Highbury-bound retire
  Threads and buses and standards with plane trees volley-
                                    ing by
And, more peculiar still, that ever-increasing spire
  Bulges over the housetops, polychromatic and high.

Stop the trolley-bus, stop !   And here, where the roads unite
  Of weariest worn-out London—no cigarettes, no beer,
No repairs undertaken, nothing in stock—alight;
  For over the waste of willow-herb, look at her, sailing
                                 clear,
A great Victorian church, tall, unbroken and bright
  In a sun that's setting in Willesden and saturating us here.

These were the streets my parents knew when they loved and
                                won—
  The brougham that crunched the gravel, the laurel-girt
                           paths that wind,

Geranium-beds for the lawn, Venetian blinds for the sun,

A separate tradesman's entrance, straw in the mews behind,

Just in the four-mile radius where hackney carriages run,

Solid Italianate houses for the solid commercial mind.

These were the streets they knew ; and I, by descent, belong

To these tall neglected houses divided into flats.

Only the church remains, where carriages used to throng

And my mother stepped out in flounces and my father stepped out in spats

To shadowy stained-glass matins or gas-lit evensong

And back in a country quiet with doffing of chimney hats.

Great red church of my parents, cruciform crossing they knew—

Over these same encaustics they and their parents trod

Bound through a red-brick transept for a once familiar pew

Where the organ set them singing and the sermon let them nod

And up this coloured brickwork the same long shadows grew

As these in the stencilled chancel where I kneel in the presence of God.

Wonder beyond Time's wonders, that Bread so white and small

Veiled in golden curtains, too mighty for men to see,

155

Is the Power which sends the shadows up this polychrome
wall,

Is God who created the present, the chain-smoking
millions and me;

Beyond the throb of the engines is the throbbing heart of
all—

Christ, at this Highbury altar, I offer myself To Thee.

Beside the Seaside

Green Shutters, shut your shutters ! Windyridge,
Let winds unnoticed whistle round your hill !
High Dormers, draw your curtains ! Slam the door,
And pack the family in the Morris eight.
Lock up the garage. Put her in reverse,
Back out with care, now, forward, off—away !
The richer people living farther out
O'ertake us in their Rovers. We, in turn,
Pass poorer families hurrying on foot
Towards the station. Very soon the town
Will echo to the groan of empty trams
And sweetshops advertise Ice Cream in vain.
Solihull, Headingley and Golders Green.
Preston and Swindon, Manchester and Leeds,
Braintree and Bocking, hear the sea ! the sea !
The smack of breakers upon windy rocks,
Spray blowing backwards from their curling walls
Of green translucent water. England leaves
Her centre for her tide-line. Father's toes,

Though now encased in coloured socks and shoes
And pressing the accelerator hard,
Ache for the feel of sand and little shrimps
To tickle in between them.   Mother vows
To be more patient with the family:
Just for its sake she will be young again.
And, at that moment, Jennifer is sick
(Over-excitement must have brought it on,
The hurried breakfast and the early start)
And Michael's rather pale, and as for Anne . . .
" Please stop a moment, Hubert, anywhere."

So evening sunlight shows us Sandy Cove
The same as last year and the year before.
Still on the brick front of the Baptist Church
SIX-THIRTY.   PREACHER :—*Mr. Pentecost—
All visitors are welcomed.*   Still the quartz
Glitters along the tops of garden walls.
Those macrocarpa still survive the gales
They must have had last winter.   Still the shops
Remain unaltered on the Esplanade—
The Circulating Library, the Stores,
Jill's Pantry, Cynthia's Ditty Box (Antiques),
Trecarrow (Maps and Souvenirs and Guides).
Still on the terrace of the big hotel

Pale pink hydrangeas turn a rusty brown
Where sea winds catch them, and yet do not die.
The bumpy lane between the tamarisks,
The escallonia hedge, and still it's there—
Our lodging-house, ten minutes from the shore.
Still unprepared to make a picnic lunch
Except by notice on the previous day.
Still nowhere for the children when it's wet
Except that smelly, overcrowded lounge.
And still no garage for the motor-car.
Still on the bedroom wall, the list of rules:
Don't waste the water. It is pumped by hand.
Don't throw old blades into the W.C.
Don't keep the bathroom long and don't be late
For meals and don't hang swim-suits out on sills
(A line has been provided at the back).
Don't empty children's sand-shoes in the hall.
Don't this, Don't that. Ah, still the same, the same
As it was last year and the year before—
But rather more expensive, now, of course.
" Anne, Jennifer and Michael—run along
Down to the sands and find yourselves some friends
While Dad and I unpack." The sea ! the sea !

   On a secluded corner of the beach

A game of rounders has been organized
By Mr. Pedder, schoolmaster and friend
Of boys and girls—particularly girls.
And here it was the tragedy began,
That life-long tragedy to Jennifer
Which ate into her soul and made her take
To secretarial work in later life
In a department of the Board of Trade.
See boys and girls assembled for the game.
Reflected in the rock pools, freckled legs
Hop, skip and jump in coltish ecstasy.
Ah ! parted lips and little pearly teeth,
Wide eyes, snub noses, shorts, divided skirts !
And last year's queen of them was Jennifer.
The snubbiest, cheekiest, lissomest of all.
One smile from her sent Mr. Pedder back
Contented to his lodgings.   She could wave
Her little finger and the elder boys
Came at her bidding.   Even tiny Ruth,
Old Lady D'Erncourt's grandchild, pet of all,
Would bring her shells as timid offerings.
So now with Anne and Michael see her stand,
Our Jennifer, our own, our last year's queen,
For this year's *début* fully confident.

" Get in your places." Heard above the waves
Are Mr. Pedder's organizing shouts.
" Come on.   Look sharp.   The tide is coming in ! "
" He hasn't seen me yet," thinks Jennifer.
" Line up your team behind you, Christabel ! "
On the wet sea-sand waiting to be seen
She stands with Anne and Michael.   Let him turn
And then he'll see me.   Let him only turn.
Smack went the tennis ball.   The bare feet ran.
And smack again.   " He's out !   Well caught, Delphine ! "
Shrieks, cartwheels, tumbling joyance of the waves.
Oh Mr. Pedder, look !   Oh here I am !
And there the three of them forlornly stood.
" You ask him, Jennifer."   " No—Michael ?—Anne ? "
" I'd rather not."   " Fains I."   " It's up to you."
" Oh, very well, then."   Timidly she goes,
Timid and proud, for the last time a child.
" Can *we* play, Mr. Pedder ? "   But his eyes
Are out to where, among the tousled heads,
He sees the golden curls of Christabel.
" Can *we* play, Mr. Pedder ? "   So he turns.
" *Who* have we here ? "   The jolly, jolly voice,
The same but not the same.   " *Who* have we here ?
The Rawlings children !   Yes, of course, you may,

Join that side, children, under Christabel."
No friendly wallop on the B.T.M.
No loving arm-squeeze and no special look.
Oh darting heart-burn, *under Christabel !*
So all those holidays the bitter truth
Sank into Jennifer.   No longer queen,
She had outgrown her strength, as Mummy said,
And Mummy made her wear these spectacles.
Because of Mummy she had lost her looks.
Had lost her looks ?   Still she was Jennifer.
The sands were still the same, the rocks the same,
The seaweed-waving pools, the bathing-cove,
The outline of the cliffs, the times of tide.
And I'm the same, of course I'm always ME.
But all that August those terrific waves
Thundered defeat along the rocky coast,
And ginger-beery surf hissed ' Christabel ! '

   Enough of tragedy !   Let wail of gulls,
The sunbows in the breakers and the breeze
Which blows the sand into the sandwiches,
Let castles crumbling in the rise of tide,
Let cool dank caves and dark interstices
Where, underneath the squelching bladderwrack,
Lurk stinging fin and sharp, marauding claw

162

Ready to pierce the rope-soled bathing-shoe,

Let darting prawn and helpless jelly-fish

Spell joy or misery to youth.   For we,

We older ones, have thoughts of higher things.

Whether we like to sit with Penguin books

In sheltered alcoves farther up the cliff,

Or to eat winkles on the Esplanade,

Or to play golf along the crowded course,

Or on a twopenny borough council chair

To doze away the strains of *Humoresque*,

Adapted for the cornet and the drums

By the conductor of the Silver Band,

Whether we own a tandem or a Rolls,

Whether we Rudge it or we trudge it, still

A single topic occupies our minds.

'Tis hinted at or boldly blazoned in

Our accents, clothes and ways of eating fish,

And being introduced and taking leave,

'Farewell,' ' So long,' ' Bunghosky,' ' Cheeribye '—

That topic all-absorbing, as it was,

Is now and ever shall be, to us—CLASS.

  Mr. and Mrs. Stephen Grosvenor-Smith

(He manages a Bank in Nottingham)

Have come to Sandy Cove for thirty years

And now they think the place is going down.

"Not what it was, I'm very much afraid.
Look at that little mite with *Attaboy*
Printed across her paper sailor hat.
Disgusting, isn't it ? Who *can* they be,
Her parents, to allow such forwardness ? "

The Browns, who thus are commented upon,
Have certainly done very well indeed.
The elder children bringing money in,
Father still working; with allowances
For this and that and little income-tax,
They probably earn seven times as much
As poor old Grosvenor-Smith. But who will grudge
Them this, their wild, spontaneous holiday ?
The morning paddle, then the mystery tour
By motor-coach inland this afternoon.
For that old mother what a happy time !
At last past bearing children, she can sit
Reposeful on a crowded bit of beach.
A week of idleness, the salty winds
Play in her greying hair; the summer sun
Puts back her freckles so that Alfred Brown
Remembers courting days in Gospel Oak
And takes her to the Flannel Dance to-night.

But all the same they think the place ' Stuck up '
And Blackpool, next year—if there *is* a next.

  And all the time the waves, the waves, the waves
Chase, intersect and flatten on the sand
As they have done for centuries, as they will
For centuries to come, when not a soul
Is left to picnic on the blazing rocks,
When England is not England, when mankind
Has blown himself to pieces.   Still the sea,
Consolingly disastrous, will return
While the strange starfish, hugely magnified,
Waits in the jewelled basin of a pool.

North Coast Recollections

No people on the golf-links, not a crack
Of well-swung driver from the fourteenth tee,
No sailing bounding ball across the turf
And lady's slipper of the fairway.   Black
Rises Bray Hill and, Stepper-wards, the sun
Sends Bray Hill's phantom stretching to the church.
The lane, the links, the beach, the cliffs are bare
The neighbourhood is dressing for a dance
And lamps are being lit in bungalows.

O ! thymy time of evening: clover scent
And feathery tamarisk round the churchyard wall
And shrivelled sea-pinks and this foreshore pale
With silver sand and sharpened quartz and slate
And brittle twigs, bleached, salted and prepared
For kindling blue-flamed fires on winter nights.

Here Petroc landed, here I stand to-day;
The same Atlantic surges roll for me
As rolled for Parson Hawker and for him,
And spent their gathering thunder on the rocks

Crashing with pebbly backwash, burst again
And strewed the nibbled fields along the cliffs.

When low tides drain the estuary gold
Small intersecting breakers far away
Ripple about a bar of shifting sand
Where centuries ago were waving woods
Where centuries hence, there will be woods again.

Within the bungalow of Mrs. Hanks
Her daughter Phoebe now French-chalks the floor.
Norman and Gordon in their dancing pumps
Slide up and down, but can't make concrete smooth.
" My Sweet Hortense . . ."
Sings louder down the garden than the sea.
" A practice record, Phoebe.   Mummykins,
Gordon and I will do the washing-up."
" We picnic here; we scrounge and help ourselves,"
Says Mrs. Hanks, and visitors will smile
To see them all turn to it.   Boys and girls
Weed in the sterile garden, mostly sand
And dead tomato-plants and chicken-runs.
To-day they cleaned the dulled Benares ware
(Dulled by the sea-mist), early made the beds,
And Phoebe twirled the icing round the cake

And Gordon tinkered with the gramophone
While into an immense enamel jug
Norman poured " Eiffel Tower " for lemonade.

O ! healthy bodies, bursting into 'teens
And bursting out of last year's summer clothes,
Fluff barking and French windows banging to
Till the asbestos walling of the place
Shakes with the life it shelters, and with all
The preparations for this evening's dance.

Now drains the colour from the convolvulus,
The windows of Trenain are flashing fire,
Black sways the tamarisk against the West,
And bathing things are taken in from sills.
One child still zig-zags homewards up the lane,
Cold on bare feet he feels the dew-wet sand.
Behind him, from a walk along the cliff,
Come pater and the mater and the dogs.

Four macrocarpa hide the tennis club.
Two children of a chartered actuary
(Beaworthy, Trouncer, Heppelwhite and Co.),
Harold and Bonzo Trouncer are engaged
In semi-finals for the tournament.
" Love thirty ! "   Pang ! across the evening air

Twangs Harold's racquet.   Plung ! the ball returns.

Experience at Budleigh Salterton

Keeps Bonzo steady at the net.   " Well done ! "

" Love forty ! "   Captain Mycroft, midst applause,

Pronounces for the Trouncers, to be sure

He can't be certain Bonzo didn't reach

A shade across the net, but Demon Sex,

That tulip figure in white cotton dress,

Bare legs, wide eyes and so tip-tilted nose

Quite overset him.   Harold serves again

And Mrs. Pardon says it's getting cold,

Miss Myatt shivers, Lady Lambourn thinks

These English evenings are a little damp

And dreams herself again in fair Shanghai.

" Game . . . AND ! and thank you ! "; so the pair from
                                                    Rock

(A neighbouring and less exclusive place)

Defeated, climb into their Morris Ten.

" The final is to-morrow !   Well, good night ! "

   He lay in wait, he lay in wait, he did,

John Lambourn, curly-headed ; dewy grass

Dampened his flannels, but he still remained.

The sunset drained the colours black and gold,

From his all-glorious First Eleven scarf.

But still he waited by the twilit hedge.

Only his eyes blazed blue with early love,
Blue blazing in the darkness of the lane,
Blue blazer, less incalculably blue,
Dark scarf, white flannels, supple body still,
First love, first light, first life.   A heartbeat noise!
His heart or little feet?   A snap of twigs
Dry, dead and brown the under branches part
And Bonzo scrambles by their secret way.
First love so deep, John Lambourn cannot speak,
So deep, he feels a tightening in his throat,
So tender, he could brush away the sand
Dried up in patches on her freckled legs,
Could hold her gently till the stars went down,
And if she cut herself would staunch the wound,
Yes, even with this First Eleven scarf,
And hold it there for hours.
So happy, and so deep he loves the world,
Could worship God and rocks and stones and trees,
Be nicer to his mother, kill himself
If that would make him pure enough for her.
And so at last he manages to say
" You going to the Hanks's hop to-night? "
" Well, I'm not sure.   Are you? "   " I think I may—
" It's pretty dud though,—only lemonade."

Sir Gawaint was a right and goodly knight
Nor ever wist he to uncurtis be.
So old, so lovely, and so very true !
Then Mrs. Wilder shut the Walter Crane
And tied the tapes and tucked her youngest in
What time without amidst the lavender
At late last ' He ' played Primula and Prue
With new-found liveliness, for bed was soon.
And in the garage, serious seventeen
Harvey, the eldest, hammered on, content,
Fixing a mizzen to his model boat.
" Coo-ee !   Coo-ee ! " across the lavender,
Across the mist of pale gypsophila
And lolling purple poppies, Mumsie called,
A splendid sunset lit the rocking-horse
And Morris pattern of the nursery walls.
" Coo-ee ! " the slate-hung, goodly-builded house
And sunset-sodden garden fell to quiet.
" Prue ! Primsie ! Mumsie wants you.   Sleepi-byes ! "
Prue jumped the marigolds and hid herself,
Her sister scampered to the Wendy Hut
And Harvey, glancing at his Ingersoll,
Thought " Damn !   I must get ready for the dance."

So on this after-storm-lit evening
To Jim the raindrops in the tamarisk,
The fuchsia bells, the sodden matchbox lid
That checked a tiny torrent in the lane
Were magnified and shining clear with life.
Then pealing out across the estuary
The Padstow bells rang up for practice-night
An undersong to birds and dripping shrubs.
The full Atlantic at September spring
Flooded a final tide-mark up the sand,
And ocean sank to silence under bells,
And the next breaker was a lesser one
Then lesser still.   Atlantic, bells and birds
Were layer on interchanging layers of sound.

A Lincolnshire Church

Greyly tremendous the thunder
Hung over the width of the wold
But here the green marsh was alight
In a huge cloud cavern of gold,
And there, on a gentle eminence,
Topping some ash trees, a tower
Silver and brown in the sunlight,
Worn by sea-wind and shower,
Lincolnshire Middle Pointed.
And around it, turning their backs,
The usual sprinkle of villas;
The usual woman in slacks,
Cigarette in her mouth,
Regretting Americans, stands
As a wireless croons in the kitchen
Manicuring her hands.
Dear old, bloody old England
Of telegraph poles and tin,
Seemingly so indifferent

And with so little soul to win.
What sort of church, I wonder ?
The path is a grassy mat,
And grass is drowning the headstones
Sloping this way and that.
" Cathedral Glass " in the windows,
A roof of unsuitable slate—
Restored with a vengeance, for certain,
About eighteen-eighty-eight.
The door swung easily open
(Unlocked, for these parts, is odd)
And there on the South aisle altar
Is the tabernacle of God.
There where the white light flickers
By the white and silver veil,
A wafer dipped in a wine-drop
Is the Presence the angels hail,
Is God who created the Heavens
And the wide green marsh as well
Who sings in the sky with the skylark
Who calls in the evening bell,
Is God who prepared His coming
With fruit of the earth for his food
With stone for building His churches

And trees for making His rood.
There where the white light flickers,
Our Creator is with us yet,
To be worshipped by you and the woman
Of the slacks and the cigarette.

*　　*　　*　　*　　*

The great door shuts, and lessens
That roar of churchyard trees
And the Presence of God Incarnate
Has brought me to my knees.
" I acknowledge my transgressions "
The well-known phrases rolled
With thunder sailing over
From the heavily clouded wold.
" And my sin is ever before me."
There in the lighted East
He stood in that lowering sunlight,
An Indian Christian priest.
And why he was here in Lincolnshire
I neither asked nor knew,
Nor whether his flock was many
Nor whether his flock was few
I thought of the heaving waters
That bore him from sun glare harsh

Of some Indian Anglican Mission
To this green enormous marsh.
There where the white light flickers,
Here, as the rains descend,
The same mysterious Godhead
Is welcoming His friend.

The Town Clerk's Views

" Yes, the Town Clerk will see you."   In I went.

He was, like all Town Clerks, from north of Trent;

A man with bye-laws busy in his head

Whose Mayor and Council followed where he led.

His most capacious brain will make us cower,

His only weakness is a lust for power—

And that is not a weakness, people think,

When unaccompanied by bribes or drink.

So let us hear this cool careerist tell

His plans to turn our country into hell.

" I cannot say how shock'd I am to see

The *variations* in our scenery.

Just take for instance, at a casual glance,

Our muddled coastline opposite to France:

Dickensian houses by the Channel tides

With old hipp'd roofs and weather-boarded sides.

I blush to think one corner of our isle

Lacks concrete villas in the modern style.

Straight lines of hops in pale brown earth of Kent,

Yeomen's square houses once, no doubt, content

With willow-bordered horse-pond, oast-house, shed,
Wide orchard, garden walls of browny-red—
All useless now, but what fine sites they'ld be
For workers' flats and some light industry.
Those lumpy church towers, unadorned with spires,
And wavy roofs that burn like smouldering fires
In sharp spring sunlight over ashen flint
Are out of date as some old aquatint.
Then glance below the line of Sussex downs
To stucco terraces of seaside towns
Turn'd into flats and residential clubs
Above the wind-slashed Corporation shrubs.
Such Georgian relics should by now, I feel,
Be all rebuilt in glass and polished steel.
Bournemouth is looking up.   I'm glad to say
That modernistic there has come to stay.
I walk the asphalt paths of Branksome Chine
In resin-scented air like strong Greek wine
And dream of cliffs of flats along those heights,
Floodlit at night with green electric lights.
But as for Dorset's flint and Purbeck stone,
Its old thatched farms in dips of down alone—
It should be merged with Hants and made to be
A self-contained and plann'd community.
Like Flint and Rutland, it is much too small

And has no reason to exist at all.
Of Devon one can hardly say the same,
But " South-West Area One " 's a better name
For those red sandstone cliffs that stain the sea
By mid-Victoria's Italy—Torquay.
And " South-West Area Two " could well include
The whole of Cornwall from Land's End to Bude.
Need I retrace my steps through other shires ?
Pinnacled Somerset ?   Northampton's spires ?
Burford's broad High Street is descending still
Stone-roofed and golden-walled her elmy hill
To meet the river Windrush.   What a shame
Her houses are not brick and all the same.
Oxford is growing up to date at last.
Cambridge, I fear, is living in the past.
She needs more factories, not useless things
Like that great chapel which they keep at King's.
As for remote East Anglia, he who searches
Finds only thatch and vast, redundant churches.
But that's the dark side.   I can safely say
A beauteous England's really on the way.
Already our hotels are pretty good
For those who're fond of *very simple food*—
Cod and two veg., free pepper, salt and mustard,

Followed by nice hard plums and lumpy custard,
A pint of bitter beer for one-and-four,
Then coffee in the lounge a shilling more.
In a few years this country will be looking
As uniform and tasty as its cooking.
Hamlets which fail to pass the planners' test
Will be demolished.   We'll rebuild the rest
To look like Welwyn mixed with Middle West.
All fields we'll turn to sports grounds, lit at night
From concrete standards by fluorescent light:
And over all the land, instead of trees,
Clean poles and wire will whisper in the breeze.
We'll keep one ancient village just to show
What England once was when the times were slow—
Broadway for me.   But here I know I must
Ask the opinion of our National Trust.
And ev'ry old cathedral that you enter
By then will be an Area Culture Centre.
Instead of nonsense about Death and Heaven
Lectures on civic duty will be given;
Eurhythmic classes dancing round the spire,
And economics courses in the choir.
So don't encourage tourists.   Stay your hand
Until we've really got the country plann'd."

Harrow-on-the-Hill

When melancholy Autumn comes to Wembley
  And electric trains are lighted after tea
The poplars near the Stadium are trembly
  With their tap and tap and whispering to me,
      Like the sound of little breakers
      Spreading out along the surf-line
When the estuary's filling
      With the sea.

Then Harrow-on-the Hill's a rocky island
  And Harrow churchyard full of sailors' graves
And the constant click and kissing of the trolley buses hissing
  Is the level to the Wealdstone turned to waves
      And the rumble of the railway
      Is the thunder of the rollers
As they gather up for plunging
      Into caves.

There's a storm cloud to the westward over Kenton,
  There's a line of harbour lights at Perivale,

Is it rounding rough Pentire in a flood of sunset fire
　　The little fleet of trawlers under sail ?
　　　Can those boats be only roof tops
　　　As they stream along the skyline
In a race for port and Padstow
　　　　With the gale ?

Verses turned
in aid of A Public Subscription (1952)
towards the restoration of the
Church of St. Katherine
Chiselhampton, Oxon

Across the wet November night
The church is bright with candlelight
　　And waiting Evensong.
A single bell with plaintive strokes
Pleads louder than the stirring oaks
　　The leafless lanes along.

It calls the choirboys from their tea
And villagers, the two or three,
　　Damp down the kitchen fire,
Let out the cat, and up the lane
Go paddling through the gentle rain
　　Of misty Oxfordshire.

How warm the many candles shine
On SAMUEL DOWBIGGIN's design

For this interior neat,
These high box pews of Georgian days
Which screen us from the public gaze
    When we make answer meet;

How gracefully their shadow falls
On bold pilasters down the walls
    And on the pulpit high.
The chandeliers would twinkle gold
As pre-Tractarian sermons roll'd
    Doctrinal, sound and dry.

From that west gallery no doubt
The viol and serpent tooted out
    The Tallis tune to Ken,
And firmly at the end of prayers
The clerk below the pulpit stairs
    Would thunder out " Amen."

But every wand'ring thought will cease
Before the noble altarpiece
    With carven swags array'd,
For there in letters all may read
The Lord's Commandments, Prayer and Creed,
    And decently display'd.

184

On country mornings sharp and clear
The penitent in faith draw near
    And kneeling here below
Partake the Heavenly Banquet spread
Of Sacramental Wine and Bread
    And JESUS' presence know.

And must that plaintive bell in vain
Plead loud along the dripping lane ?
    And must the building fall ?
Not while we love the Church and live
And of our charity will give
    Our much, our more, our all.

Sunday Morning, King's Cambridge

File into yellow candle light, fair choristers of King's

    Lost in the shadowy silence of canopied Renaissance stalls

In blazing glass above the dark glow skies and thrones and
                                    wings

    Blue, ruby, gold and green between the whiteness of the
                                      walls

And with what rich precision the stonework soars and
                                      springs

    To fountain out a spreading vault—a shower that never
                                      falls.

The white of windy Cambridge courts, the cobbles brown
                                   and dry,

    The gold of plaster Gothic with ivy overgrown,

The apple-red, the silver fronts, the wide green flats and
                                      high,

    The yellowing elm-trees circled out on islands of their
                                    own—

Oh, here behold all colours change that catch the flying sky

    To waves of pearly light that heave along the shafted
                                      stone.

In far East Anglian churches, the clasped hands lying long

Recumbent on sepulchral slabs or effigied in brass

Buttress with prayer this vaulted roof so white and light
and strong

And countless congregations as the generations pass

Join choir and great crowned organ case, in centuries of song

To praise Eternity contained in Time and coloured glass.

Christmas

The bells of waiting Advent ring,
   The Tortoise stove is lit again
And lamp-oil light across the night
   Has caught the streaks of winter rain
In many a stained-glass window sheen
From Crimson Lake to Hooker's Green.

The holly in the windy hedge
   And round the Manor House the yew
Will soon be stripped to deck the ledge,
   The altar, font and arch and pew,
So that the villagers can say
" The church looks nice " on Christmas Day.

Provincial public houses blaze
   And Corporation tramcars clang,
On lighted tenements I gaze
   Where paper decorations hang,
And bunting in the red Town Hall
Says " Merry Christmas to you all."

And London shops on Christmas Eve
   Are strung with silver bells and flowers
As hurrying clerks the City leave
   To pigeon-haunted classic towers,
And marbled clouds go scudding by
The many-steepled London sky.

And girls in slacks remember Dad,
   And oafish louts remember Mum,
And sleepless children's hearts are glad,
   And Christmas-morning bells say " Come ! "
Even to shining ones who dwell
Safe in the Dorchester Hotel.

And is it true ?   And is it true,
   This most tremendous tale of all,
Seen in a stained-glass window's hue,
   A Baby in an ox's stall ?
The Maker of the stars and sea
Become a Child on earth for me ?

And is it true ?   For if it is,
   No loving fingers tying strings
Around those tissued fripperies,
   The sweet and silly Christmas things,

Bath salts and inexpensive scent
And hideous tie so kindly meant,

No love that in a family dwells,
   No carolling in frosty air,
Nor all the steeple-shaking bells
   Can with this single Truth compare—
That God was Man in Palestine
And lives to-day in Bread and Wine.

The Licorice Fields at Pontefract

In the licorice fields at Pontefract
   My love and I did meet
And many a burdened licorice bush
   Was blooming round our feet;
Red hair she had and golden skin,
Her sulky lips were shaped for sin,
Her sturdy legs were flannel-slack'd,
The strongest legs in Pontefract.

The light and dangling licorice flowers
   Gave off the sweetest smells;
From various black Victorian towers
   The Sunday evening bells
Came pealing over dales and hills
And tanneries and silent mills
And lowly streets where country stops
And little shuttered corner shops.

She cast her blazing eyes on me
   And plucked a licorice leaf;

I was her captive slave and she
   My red-haired robber chief.
Oh love ! for love I could not speak,
It left me winded, wilting, weak
And held in brown arms strong and bare
And wound with flaming ropes of hair.

Church of England thoughts
occasioned by hearing the bells
of Magdalen Tower
from the Botanic Garden, Oxford
on St. Mary Magdalen's Day

I see the urn against the yew,
  The sunlit urn of sculptured stone,
I see its shapely shadow fall
On this enormous garden wall
  Which makes a kingdom of its own.

A grassy kingdom sweet to view
  With tiger lilies still in flower
And beds of umbelliferæ
Ranged in Linnaean symmetry,
  All in the sound of Magdalen tower.

A multiplicity of bells,
  A changing cadence, rich and deep
Swung from those pinnacles on high
To fill the trees and flood the sky
  And rock the sailing clouds to sleep.

A Church of England sound, it tells
  Of " moderate " worship, God and State,
Where matins congregations go
Conservative and good and slow
  To elevations of the plate.

And loud through resin-scented chines
  And purple rhododendrons roll'd,
I hear the bells for Eucharist
From churches blue with incense mist
  Where reredoses twinkle gold.

Chapels-of-ease by railway lines
  And humble streets and smells of gas
I hear your plaintive ting-tangs call
From many a gabled western wall
  To Morning Prayer or Holy Mass.

In country churches old and pale
  I hear the changes smoothly rung
And watch the coloured sallies fly
From rugged hands to rafters high
  As round and back the bells are swung.

194

Before the spell begin to fail,
  Before the bells have lost their power,
Before the grassy kingdom fade
And Oxford traffic roar invade,
  I thank the bells of Magdalen Tower.

Essex

" The vagrant visitor erstwhile,"
　My colour-plate book says to me,
" Could wend by hedgerow-side and stile,
　From Benfleet down to Leigh-on-Sea."

And as I turn the colour-plates
　Edwardian Essex opens wide,
Mirrored in ponds and seen through gates,
　Sweet uneventful countryside.

Like streams the little by-roads run
　Through oats and barley round a hill
To where blue willows catch the sun
　By some white weather-boarded mill.

" A Summer Idyll Matching Tye "
　" At Havering-atte-Bower, the Stocks "
And cobbled pathways lead the eye
　To cottage doors and hollyhocks.

Far Essex,—fifty miles away
　　The level wastes of sucking mud
Where distant barges high with hay
　　Come sailing in upon the flood.

Near Essex of the River Lea
　　And anglers out with hook and worm
And Epping Forest glades where we
　　Had beanfeasts with my father's firm.

At huge and convoluted pubs
　　They used to set us down from brakes
In that half-land of football clubs
　　Which London near the Forest makes.

The deepest Essex few explore
　　Where steepest thatch is sunk in flowers
And out of elm and sycamore
　　Rise flinty fifteenth-century towers.

I see the little branch line go
　　By white farms roofed in red and brown,
The old Great Eastern winding slow
　　To some forgotten country town.

197

Now yarrow chokes the railway track,
  Brambles obliterate the stile,
No motor coach can take me back
  To that Edwardian " erstwhile ".

Huxley Hall

In the Garden City Café with its murals on the wall
Before a talk on " Sex and Civics " I meditated on the Fall.

Deep depression settled on me under that electric glare
While outside the lightsome poplars flanked the rose-beds
in the square.

While outside the carefree children sported in the summer
haze
And released their inhibitions in a hundred different ways.

She who eats her greasy crumpets snugly in the inglenook
Of some birch-enshrouded homestead, dropping butter on
her book

Can she know the deep depression of this bright, hygienic
hell ?
And her husband, stout free-thinker, can he share in it as
well ?

Not the folk-museum's charting of man's Progress out of
slime

199

Can release me from the painful seeming accident of Time.

Barry smashes Shirley's dolly, Shirley's eyes are crossed
with hate,
Comrades plot a Comrade's downfall " in the interests of
the State ".

Not my vegetarian dinner, not my lime-juice minus gin,
Quite can drown a faint conviction that we may be born
in Sin.

House of Rest

Now all the world she knew is dead
  In this small room she lives her days
The wash-hand stand and single bed
  Screened from the public gaze.

The horse-brass shines, the kettle sings,
  The cup of China tea
Is tasted among cared-for things
  Ranged round for me to see—

Lincoln, by Valentine and Co.,
  Now yellowish brown and stained,
But there some fifty years ago
  Her Harry was ordained;

Outside the Church at Woodhall Spa
  The smiling groom and bride,
And here's his old tobacco jar
  Dried lavender inside.

201

I do not like to ask if he
    Was " High " or " Low " or " Broad "
Lest such a question seem to be
    A mockery of Our Lord.

Her full grey eyes look far beyond
    The little room and me
To village church and village pond
    And ample rectory.

She sees her children each in place
    Eyes downcast as they wait,
She hears her Harry murmur Grace,
    Then heaps the porridge plate.

Aroused at seven, to bed by ten,
    They fully lived each day,
Dead sons, so motor-bike-mad then,
    And daughters far away.

Now when the bells for Eucharist
    Sound in the Market Square,
With sunshine struggling through the mist
    And Sunday in the air,

202

The veil between her and her dead
　　Dissolves and shows them clear,
The Consecration Prayer is said
　　And all of them are near.

Middlesex

Gaily into Ruislip Gardens
    Runs the red electric train,
With a thousand Ta's and Pardon's
    Daintily alights Elaine;
Hurries down the concrete station
With a frown of concentration,
Out into the outskirt's edges
Where a few surviving hedges
Keep alive our lost Elysium—rural Middlesex again.

Well cut Windsmoor flapping lightly,
    Jacqmar scarf of mauve and green
Hiding hair which, Friday nightly,
    Delicately drowns in Drene;
Fair Elaine the bobby-soxer,
Fresh-complexioned with Innoxa,
Gains the garden—father's hobby—
Hangs her Windsmoor in the lobby,
Settles down to sandwich supper and the television screen.

Gentle Brent, I used to know you

    Wandering Wembley-wards at will,

Now what change your waters show you

    In the meadowlands you fill !

Recollect the elm-trees misty

And the footpaths climbing twisty

Under cedar-shaded palings,

Low laburnum-leaned-on railings,

Out of Northolt on and upward to the heights
                    of Harrow hill.

Parish of enormous hayfields

    Perivale stood all alone,

And from Greenford scent of mayfields

    Most enticingly was blown

Over market gardens tidy,

Taverns for the *bona fide*,

Cockney anglers, cockney shooters,

Murray Poshes, Lupin Pooters

Long in Kensal Green and Highgate silent under
                    soot and stone.

Seaside Golf

How straight it flew, how long it flew.
   It clear'd the rutty track
And soaring, disappeared from view
   Beyond the bunker's back—
A glorious, sailing, bounding drive
That made me glad I was alive.

And down the fairway, far along
   It glowed a lonely white;
I played an iron sure and strong
   And clipp'd it out of sight,
And spite of grassy banks between
I knew I'd find it on the green.

And so I did.   It lay content
   Two paces from the pin;
A steady putt and then it went
   Oh, most securely in.
The very turf rejoiced to see
That quite unprecedented three.

Ah ! seaweed smells from sandy caves
   And thyme and mist in whiffs,
In-coming tide, Atlantic waves
   Slapping the sunny cliffs,
Lark song and sea sounds in the air
And splendour, splendour everywhere.

I.M.
Walter Ramsden
ob. March 26, 1947
Pembroke College, Oxford

Dr. Ramsden cannot read *The Times* obituary to-day
  He's dead.
Let monographs on silk worms by other people be
  Thrown away
  Unread
For he who best could understand and criticize them, he
  Lies clay
  In bed.

The body waits in Pembroke College where the ivy taps the
                                                        panes
    All night;
That old head so full of knowledge, that good heart that
                                              kept the brains
    All right,
Those old cheeks that faintly flushed as the port suffused
                                              the veins,
    Drain'd white.

208

Crocus in the Fellows' Garden, winter jasmine up the wall
  Gleam gold.
Shadows of Victorian chimneys on the sunny grassplot fall
  Long, cold.
Master, Bursar, Senior Tutor, these, his three survivors, all
  Feel old.

They remember, as the coffin to its final obsequations
  Leaves the gates,
Buzz of bees in window boxes on their summer minis-
                                               trations,
  Kitchen din,
  Cups and plates,
And the getting of bump suppers for the long-dead genera-
                                               tions
  Coming in,
  From Eights.

Norfolk

How did the Devil come ? When first attack ?
    These Norfolk lanes recall lost innocence,
The years fall off and find me walking back
    Dragging a stick along the wooden fence
Down this same path, where, forty years ago,
My father strolled behind me, calm and slow.

I used to fill my hand with sorrel seeds
    And shower him with them from the tops of stiles,
I used to butt my head into his tweeds
    To make him hurry down those languorous miles
Of ash and alder-shaded lanes, till here
Our moorings and the masthead would appear.

There after supper lit by lantern light
    Warm in the cabin I could lie secure
And hear against the polished sides at night
    The lap lap lapping of the weedy Bure,
A whispering and watery Norfolk sound
Telling of all the moonlit reeds around.

How did the Devil come ?   When first attack ?

   The church is just the same, though now I know

Fowler of Louth restored it.   Time, bring back

   The rapturous ignorance of long ago,

The peace, before the dreadful daylight starts,

Of unkept promises and broken hearts.

The Metropolitan Railway
BAKER STREET STATION BUFFET

Early Electric !   With what radiant hope
   Men formed this many-branched electrolier,
Twisted the flex around the iron rope
   And let the dazzling vacuum globes hang clear,
And then with hearts the rich contrivance fill'd
Of copper, beaten by the Bromsgrove Guild.

Early Electric !   Sit you down and see,
   'Mid this fine woodwork and a smell of dinner,
A stained-glass windmill and a pot of tea,
   And sepia views of leafy lanes in PINNER,—
Then visualize, far down the shining lines,
Your parents' homestead set in murmuring pines.

Smoothly from HARROW, passing PRESTON ROAD,
   They saw the last green fields and misty sky,
At NEASDEN watched a workmen's train unload,
   And, with the morning villas sliding by,

212

They felt so sure on their electric trip
That Youth and Progress were in partnership.

And all that day in murky London Wall
　　The thought of RUISLIP kept him warm inside;
At FARRINGDON that lunch hour at a stall
　　He bought a dozen plants of London Pride;
While she, in arc-lit Oxford Street adrift,
Soared through the sales by safe hydraulic lift.

Early Electric !　Maybe even here
　　They met that evening at six-fifteen
Beneath the hearts of this electrolier
　　And caught the first non-stop to WILLESDEN GREEN,
Then out and on, through rural RAYNER'S LANE
To autumn-scented Middlesex again.

Cancer has killed him.　Heart is killing her.
　　The trees are down.　An Odeon flashes fire
Where stood their villa by the murmuring fir
　　When " they would for their children's good conspire."
Of all their loves and hopes on hurrying feet
Thou art the worn memorial, Baker Street.

213

Late-Flowering Lust

My head is bald, my breath is bad,
  Unshaven is my chin,
I have not now the joys I had
  When I was young in sin.

I run my fingers down your dress
  With brandy-certain aim
And you respond to my caress
  And maybe feel the same.

But I've a picture of my own
  On this reunion night,
Wherein two skeletons are shewn
  To hold each other tight;

Dark sockets look on emptiness
  Which once was loving-eyed,
The mouth that opens for a kiss
  Has got no tongue inside.

I cling to you inflamed with fear
    As now you cling to me,
I feel how frail you are my dear
    And wonder what will be—

A week ? or twenty years remain ?
    And then—what kind of death ?
A losing fight with frightful pain
    Or a gasping fight for breath ?

Too long we let our bodies cling,
    We cannot hide disgust
At all the thoughts that in us spring
    From this late-flowering lust.

Sun and Fun

I walked into the night-club in the morning;
  There was kummel on the handle of the door.
The ashtrays were unemptied,
The cleaning unattempted,
  And a squashed tomato sandwich on the floor.

I pulled aside the thick magenta curtains
  —So Regency, so Regency, my dear—
And a host of little spiders
Ran a race across the ciders
  To a box of baby 'pollies by the beer.

Oh sun upon the summer-going by-pass
  Where ev'rything is speeding to the sea,
And wonder beyond wonder
That here where lorries thunder
  The sun should ever percolate to me.

216

When Boris used to call in his Sedanca,
  When Teddy took me down to his estate
When my nose excited passion,
When my clothes were in the fashion,
  When my beaux were never cross if I was late,

There was sun enough for lazing upon beaches,
  There was fun enough for far into the night.
But I'm dying now and done for,
What on earth was all the fun for?
  For I'm old and ill and terrified and tight.

Original Sin on the Sussex Coast

Now on this out of season afternoon
Day schools which cater for the sort of boy
Whose parents go by Pullman once a month
To do a show in town, pour out their young
Into the sharply red October light.
Here where The Drive and Buckhurst Road converge
I watch the rival gangs and am myself
A schoolboy once again in shivering shorts.
I see the dust of sherbet on the chin
Of Andrew Knox well-dress'd, well-born, well-fed,
Even at nine a perfect gentleman,
Willie Buchanan waiting at his side—
Another Scot, eruptions on his skin.
I hear Jack Drayton whistling from the fence
Which hides the copper domes of " Cooch Behar ".
That was the signal.   So there's no escape.
A race for Willow Way and jump the hedge
Behind the Granville Bowling Club ?   Too late.
They'll catch me coming out in Seapink Lane.

Across the Garden of Remembrance ?   No,

That would be blasphemy and bring bad luck.

Well then, I'm *for* it.   Andrew's at me first,

He pinions me in that especial grip

His brother learned in Kobë from a Jap

(No chance for me against the Japanese).

Willie arrives and winds me with a punch

Plum in the tummy, grips the other arm.

" You're to be booted.   Hold him steady, chaps ! "

A wait for taking aim.   Oh trees and sky !

Then crack against the column of my spine,

Blackness and breathlessness and sick with pain

I stumble on the asphalt.   Off they go

Away, away, thank God, and out of sight

So that I lie quite still and climb to sense

Too out of breath and strength to make a sound.

   Now over Polegate vastly sets the sun;

Dark rise the Downs from darker looking elms,

And out of Southern railway trains to tea

Run happy boys down various Station Roads,

Satchels of homework jogging on their backs,

So trivial and so healthy in the shade

Of these enormous Downs.   And when they're home,

When the Post-Toasties mixed with Golden Shred

Make for the kiddies such a scrumptious feast,
Does Mum, the Persil-user, still believe
That there's no Devil and that youth is bliss ?
As certain as the sun behind the Downs
And quite as plain to see, the Devil walks.

Devonshire Street W.1

The heavy mahogany door with its wrought-iron screen
    Shuts.   And the sound is rich, sympathetic, discreet.
The sun still shines on this eighteenth-century scene
    With Edwardian faience adornments—Devonshire Street

No hope.   And the X-ray photographs under his arm
    Confirm the message.   His wife stands timidly by.
The opposite brick-built house looks lofty and calm
    Its chimneys steady against a mackerel sky.

No hope.   And the iron nob of this palisade
    So cold to the touch, is luckier now than he
" Oh merciless, hurrying Londoners !   Why was I made
    For the long and the painful deathbed coming to me ? "

She puts her fingers in his as, loving and silly,
    At long-past Kensington dances she used to do
" It's cheaper to take the tube to Piccadilly
    And then we can catch a nineteen or a twenty-two."

The Cottage Hospital

At the end of a long-walled garden
  in a red provincial town,
A brick path led to a mulberry—
  scanty grass at its feet.
I lay under blackening branches
  where the mulberry leaves hung down
Sheltering ruby fruit globes
  from a Sunday-tea-time heat.
Apple and plum espaliers
  basked upon bricks of brown;
The air was swimming with insects,
  and children played in the street.

Out of this bright intentness
  into the mulberry shade
Musca domestica (housefly)
  swung from the August light
Slap into slithery rigging
  by the waiting spider made

Which spun the lithe elastic
   till the fly was shrouded tight.
Down came the hairy talons
   and horrible poison blade
And none of the garden noticed
   that fizzing, hopeless fight.

Say in what Cottage Hospital
   whose pale green walls resound
With the tap upon polished parquet
   of inflexible nurses' feet
Shall I myself be lying
   when they range the screens around ?
And say shall I groan in dying,
   as I twist the sweaty sheet ?
Or gasp for breath uncrying,
   as I feel my senses drown'd
While the air is swimming with insects
   and children play in the street ?

A Child Ill

Oh, little body, do not die.
  The soul looks out through wide blue eyes
So questioningly into mine,
  That my tormented soul replies:

" Oh, little body, do not die.
  You hold the soul that talks to me
Although our conversation be
  As wordless as the windy sky."

So looked my father at the last
  Right in my soul, before he died,
Though words we spoke went heedless past
  As London traffic-roar outside.

And now the same blue eyes I see
  Look through me from a little son,
So questioning, so searchingly
  That youthfulness and age are one.

My father looked at me and died
  Before my soul made full reply.
Lord, leave this other Light alight—
  Oh, little body, do not die.

Business Girls

From the geyser ventilators
    Autumn winds are blowing down
On a thousand business women
    Having baths in Camden Town.

Waste pipes chuckle into runnels,
    Steam's escaping here and there,
Morning trains through Camden cutting
    Shake the Crescent and the Square.

Early nip of changeful autumn,
    Dahlias glimpsed through garden doors,
At the back precarious bathrooms
    Jutting out from upper floors;

And behind their frail partitions
    Business women lie and soak,
Seeing through the draughty skylight
    Flying clouds and railway smoke.

Rest you there, poor unbelov'd ones,
　Lap your loneliness in heat.
All too soon the tiny breakfast,
　Trolley-bus and windy street !

Remorse

The lungs draw in the air and rattle it out again;
  The eyes revolve in their sockets and upwards stare;
No more worry and waiting and troublesome doubt again—
  She whom I loved and left is no longer there.

The nurse puts down her knitting and walks across to her,
  With quick professional eye she surveys the dead.
Just one patient the less and little the loss to her,
  Distantly tender she settles the shrunken head.

Protestant claims and Catholic, the wrong and the right
                                               of them,
  Unimportant they seem in the face of death—
But my neglect and unkindness—to lose the sight of them
  I would listen even again to that labouring breath.

The Old Liberals

Pale green of the *English Hymnal* ! Yattendon hymns
  Played on the *hautbois* by a lady dress'd in blue
  Her white-hair'd father accompanying her thereto
On tenor or bass-recorder. Daylight swims
  On sectional bookcase, delicate cup and plate
  And William de Morgan tiles around the grate
And many the silver birches the pearly light shines through.

I think such a running together of woodwind sound,
  Such painstaking piping high on a Berkshire hill,
  Is sad as an English autumn heavy and still,
Sad as a country silence, tractor-drowned;
For deep in the hearts of the man and the woman playing
  The rose of a world that was not has withered away.
Where are the wains with garlanded swathes a-swaying ?
Where are the swains to wend through the lanes a-maying ?
  Where are the blithe and jocund to ted the hay ?
  Where are the free folk of England ? Where are they ?

Ask of the Abingdon bus with full load creeping
   Down into denser suburbs.   The birch lets go
   But one brown leaf upon browner bracken below.
Ask of the cinema manager.   Night airs die
To still, ripe scent of the fungus and wet woods weeping.
   Ask at the fish and chips in the Market Square.
   Here amid firs and a final sunset flare
Recorder and *hautbois* only moan at a mouldering sky.

Greenaway

I know so well this turfy mile,
   These clumps of sea-pink withered brown,
The breezy cliff, the awkward stile,
   The sandy path that takes me down.

To crackling layers of broken slate
   Where black and flat sea-woodlice crawl
And isolated rock pools wait
   Wash from the highest tides of all.

I know the roughly blasted track
   That skirts a small and smelly bay
And over squelching bladderwrack
   Leads to the beach at Greenaway.

Down on the shingle safe at last
   I hear the slowly dragging roar
As mighty rollers mount to cast
   Small coal and seaweed on the shore,

And spurting far as it can reach
  The shooting surf comes hissing round
To heave a line along the beach
  Of cowries waiting to be found.

Tide after tide by night and day
  The breakers battle with the land
And rounded smooth along the bay
  The faithful rocks protecting stand.

But in a dream the other night
  I saw this coastline from the sea
And felt the breakers plunging white
  Their weight of waters over me.

There were the stile, the turf, the shore,
  The safety line of shingle beach
With every stroke I struck the more
  The backwash sucked me out of reach.

Back into what a water-world
  Of waving weed and waiting claws ?
Of writhing tentacles uncurled
  To drag me to what dreadful jaws ?

232

The Olympic Girl

The sort of girl I like to see
Smiles down from her great height at me.
She stands in strong, athletic pose
And wrinkles her *retroussé* nose.
Is it distaste that makes her frown,
So furious and freckled, down
On an unhealthy worm like me ?
Or am I what she likes to see ?
I do not know, though much I care.
εἴθε γενοίμην . . . would I were
(Forgive me, shade of Rupert Brooke)
An object fit to claim her look.
Oh ! would I were her racket press'd
With hard excitement to her breast
And swished into the sunlit air
Arm-high above her tousled hair,
And banged against the bounding ball
" Oh ! Plung ! " my tauten'd strings would call,
" Oh ! Plung ! my darling, break my strings

233

For you I will do brilliant things."
And when the match is over, I
Would flop beside you, hear you sigh;
And then, with what supreme caress,
You'ld tuck me up into my press.
Fair tigress of the tennis courts,
So short in sleeve and strong in shorts,
Little, alas, to you I mean,
For I am bald and old and green.

The Dear Old Village

The dear old village ! *Lin-lan-lone* the bells
(Which should be six) ring over hills and dells,
But since the row about the ringers' tea
It's *lin-lan-lone*. They're only ringing three.
The elm leaves patter like a summer shower
As *lin-lan-lone* pours through them from the tower.
From that embattled, lichen-crusted fane
Which scoops the sun into each western pane,
The bells ring over hills and dells in vain.
For we are free to-day. No need to praise
The Unseen Author of our nights and days;
No need to hymn the rich uncurling spring
For DYKES is nowhere half so good as BING.
Nature is out of date and GOD is too;
Think what atomic energy can do !

Farmers have wired the public rights-of-way
Should any wish to walk to church to pray.
Along the village street the sunset strikes
On young men tuning up their motor-bikes,

235

And country girls with lips and nails vermilion
Wait, nylon-legged, to straddle on the pillion.
Off to the roadhouse and the Tudor Bar
And then the Sunday-opened cinema.
While to the church's iron-studded door
Go two old ladies and a child of four.

    This is the age of progress.   Let us meet
The new progressives of the village street.
Hear not the water lapsing down the rills,
Lift not your eyes to the surrounding hills,
While spring recalls the miracle of birth
Let us, for heaven's sake, keep down to earth.

    See that square house, late Georgian and smart,
Two fields away it proudly stands apart,
Dutch barn and concrete cow-sheds have replaced
The old thatched roofs which once the yard disgraced
Here wallows Farmer WHISTLE in his riches,
His ample stomach heaved above his breeches.
You'd never think that in such honest beef
Lurk'd an adulterous braggart, liar and thief.
His wife brought with her thirty-thousand down:
He keeps his doxy in the nearest town.
No man more anxious on the R.D.C.
For better rural cottages than he,

Especially when he had some land to sell
Which, as a site, would suit the Council well.
So three times what he gave for it he got,
For one undrainable and useless plot
Where now the hideous Council houses stand.
Unworked on and unworkable their land,
The wind blows under each unseason'd door,
The floods pour over every kitchen floor,
And country wit, which likes to laugh at sin,
Christens the Council houses " Whistle's Win."
Woe to some lesser farmer who may try
To call his bluff or to expose his lie.
Remorseless as a shark in London's City,
He gets at them through the War Ag. Committee.

   He takes no part in village life beyond
Throwing his refuse in a neighbour's pond
And closing footpaths, not repairing walls,
Leaving a cottage till at last it falls.
People protest.   A law-suit then begins,
But as he's on the Bench, he always wins.

   Behind rank elders, shadowing a pool,
And near the Church, behold the Village School,
Its gable rising out of ivy thick
Shows " Eighteen-Sixty " worked in coloured brick.

By nineteen-forty-seven, hurrah ! hooray
This institution has outlived its day.
In the bad times of old feudality
The villagers were ruled by masters three—
Squire, parson, schoolmaster.   Of these, the last
Knew best the village present and its past.
Now, I am glad to say, the man is dead,
The children have a motor-bus instead,
And in a town eleven miles away
We train them to be " Citizens of To-day."
And many a cultivated hour they pass
In a fine school with walls of vita-glass.
Civics, eurhythmics, economics, Marx,
How-to-respect-wild-life-in-National-Parks;
Plastics, gymnastics—thus they learn to scorn
The old thatch'd cottages where they were born.
The girls, ambitious to begin their lives
Serving in WOOLWORTH'S, rather than as wives;
The boys, who cannot yet escape the land,
At driving tractors lend a clumsy hand.
An eight-hour day for all, and more than three
Of these are occupied in making tea
And talking over what we all agree—
Though " Music while you work " is now our wont,

It's not so nice as " Music while you don't."
Squire, parson, schoolmaster turn in their graves.
And *let* them turn.   We are no longer slaves.

  So much for youth.   I fear we older folk
Must be dash'd off with a more hurried stroke.
Old Mrs. SPEAK has cut, for fifteen years,
Her husband's widowed sister Mrs. SHEARS,
Though how she's managed it, I cannot say,
Sharing a cottage with her night and day.
What caused the quarrel fifteen years ago
And how BERT SPEAK gets on, I do not know,
There the three live in that old dwelling quaint
Which water-colourists delight to paint.
Of the large brood round Mrs. COKER's door,
Coker has definitely fathered four
And two are Farmer Whistle's: two they say
Have coloured fathers in the U.S.A.
I learn'd all this and more from Mrs. FREE,
Pride of the Women's Institute is she,
Says " Sir " or " Madam " to you, knows her station
And how to make a quiet insinuation.
The unrespectable must well know why
They fear her lantern jaw and leaden eye.

  There is no space to tell about the chaps—

Which pinch, which don't, which beat their wives
with straps.

Go to the Inn on any Friday night

And listen to them while they're getting tight

At the expense of him who stands them drinks,

The Mass-Observer with the Hillman Minx.

(Unwitting he of all the knowing winks)

The more he circulates the bitter ales

The longer and the taller grow the tales.

" Ah ! this is England," thinks he, " rich and pure

As tilth and loam and wains and horse-manure,

Slow—yes.   But sociologically sound."

" Landlord ! " he cries, " the same again all round ! "

The Village Inn

" The village inn, the dear old inn,
So ancient, clean and free from sin,
True centre of our rural life
Where Hodge sits down beside his wife
And talks of Marx and nuclear fission
With all a rustic's intuition.
Ah, more than church or school or hall,
The village inn's the heart of all."
So spake the brewer's P.R.O.,
A man who really ought to know,
For he is paid for saying so.
And then he kindly gave to me
A lovely coloured booklet free.
'Twas full of prose that sang the praise
Of coaching inns in Georgian days,
Showing how public-houses are
More modern than the motor-car,
More English than the weald or wold
And almost equally as old,

And run for love and not for gold
Until I felt a filthy swine
For loathing beer and liking wine,
And rotten to the very core
For thinking village inns a bore,
And village bores more sure to roam
To village inns than stay at home.
And then I thought I *must* be wrong,
So up I rose and went along
To that old village alehouse where
In neon lights is written " Bear ".

Ah, where's the inn that once I knew
    With brick and chalky wall
Up which the knobbly pear-tree grew
    For fear the place would fall ?

Oh, that old pot-house isn't there,
    It wasn't worth our while ;
You'll find we have rebuilt " The Bear "
    In Early Georgian style.

But winter jasmine used to cling
    With golden stars a-shine
Where rain and wind would wash and swing
    The crudely painted sign.

242

And where's the roof of golden thatch ?
    The chimney-stack of stone ?
The crown-glass panes that used to match
    Each sunset with their own ?

Oh now the walls are red and smart,
    The roof has emerald tiles.
The neon sign's a work of art
    And visible for miles.

The bar inside was papered green,
    The settles grained like oak,
The only light was paraffin,
    The woodfire used to smoke.

And photographs from far and wide
    Were hung around the room:
The hunt, the church, the football side,
    And Kitchener of Khartoum.

Our air-conditioned bars are lined
    With washable material,
The stools are steel, the taste refined,
    Hygienic and ethereal.

Hurrah, hurrah, for hearts of oak !
Away with inhibitions !
For here's a place to sit and soak
In sanit'ry conditions.

Station Syren

She sat with a Warwick Deeping,
   Her legs curl'd round in a ring,
Like a beautiful panther sleeping,
   Yet always ready to spring.

Tweed on her well-knit torso,
   Silk on each big strong leg,
An officer's lady—and more so
   Than those who buy off the peg.

More cash than she knew of for spending
   As a Southgate girl at home,
For there's crooning and clinging unending
   For the queen of the girls at the 'drome.

Beautiful brown eyes burning
   Deep on the Deeping page,
Beautiful dark hair learning
   Coiffuring tricks of the age.

Negligent hand for holding
   A Flight-Lieutenant at bay,
Petulant lips for scolding
   And kissing the trouble away

But she isn't exactly partial
   To any of that sort of thing,
So maybe the Air Vice-Marshal
   Will buy her a Bravington ring.

Hunter Trials

It's awf'lly bad luck on Diana,
 Her ponies have swallowed their bits;
She fished down their throats with a spanner
 And frightened them all into fits.

So now she's attempting to borrow.
 Do lend her some bits, Mummy, *do*;
I'll lend her my own for to-morrow,
 But to-day *I*'ll be wanting them too.

Just look at Prunella on Guzzle,
 The wizardest pony on earth;
Why doesn't she slacken his muzzle
 And tighten the breech in his girth?

I say, Mummy, there's Mrs. Geyser
 And doesn't she look pretty sick?
I bet it's because Mona Lisa
 Was hit on the hock with a brick.

Miss Blewitt says Monica threw it,
　　But Monica says it was Joan,
And Joan's very thick with Miss Blewitt,
　　So Monica's sulking alone.

And Margaret failed in her paces,
　　Her withers got tied in a noose,
So her coronets caught in the traces
　　And now all her fetlocks are loose.

Oh, it's me now.　I'm terribly nervous.
　　I wonder if Smudges will shy.
She's practically certain to swerve as
　　Her Pelham is over one eye.

　　　*　　*　　*　　*　　*

Oh wasn't it naughty of Smudges ?
　　Oh, Mummy, I'm sick with disgust.
She threw me in front of the Judges,
　　And my silly old collarbone's bust.

A Literary Discovery

Sent to the Editor of *Time and Tide*, Dec. 1952

Dear Sir,

I was lately in a second-hand bookshop in East Grinstead and bought for fourpence a green cloth and gilt-edged edition of Longfellow's poems (Crown octavo, Ward Lock & Co., London, 1875). Witness my surprise when I found inside it a piece of yellowish cream-laid paper (water-mark Mudie's Libraries—Swedenborg Bond) with a manuscript poem. There was no surname in the flyleaf of the book, but an inscription read, " To Ellen from her loving husband." The poem was certainly in the same hand as the inscription, a sloping rather clerkly fist suggesting long hours practising pothooks. Seeing that the verses refer to the celebrated novelist Mrs. Henry Wood (1814–1887) whose Christian name was Ellen, I hazard the guess that it is the work of her husband Henry Wood whom she married in 1836. The poem was placed in the leaves where " The Belfry at Bruges " appeared whose famous opening line requires Bruges to be pronounced as two syllables, American style, to obtain full beauty.

' In the market place of Bruges stands the belfry old and brown.'

Not far off is a similar poem " Nüremberg ", imparting factual information of a most inspiring kind

from the guide-book.   I quote a few stanzas from
" Nüremberg " for it seems to have influenced the
poet of the verses I have found :

In the Courtyard of the castle, bound with many an iron band,
Stands the mighty linden planted by Queen Cunigunde's hand, . . .

Here, when Art was still religion, with a simple reverent heart,
Lived and laboured Albrecht Dürer, the Evangelist of Art ;

Here Hans Sachs, the cobbler-poet, laureate of the gentle craft,
Wisest of the Twelve Wise Masters, in huge folios sang and
laughed.

I am hoping that some readers, as scholarly as I
am, will be able to throw some light on the verses
that follow.   Important questions are raised.   Did
the Henry Woods ever live at Gomshall ?   When
did Longfellow visit them ?   Did Henry Wood
survive his visit ?   Was the house renamed ?   With
the idea of helping other scholars, I have annotated
the verses.   I may say that, if you do not see fit
to print this, I shall send it to *The Times Literary
Supplement* where it will, no doubt, be published on
that interesting back page.

*   *   *

Where yon crenellated mansion on the hill surmounts the
pines,

Many a long-departed merchant[1] in the cellar stored his
wines,

Hock for fish,[2] for pheasant claret, as the sun sloped slowly
down

Over ambient lawns and pinewoods backed beyond by
Guildford town.

Once the railway out of London over twenty years ago[3]

To that crenellated mansion brought the poet Longfellow.

There were footmen to receive him, and a butler, stern as
doom

Led him by the beetling antlers[4] to the large withdrawing
room.

She was waiting to receive him, by her side her husband
stood

Who alive would see the husband ?[5] this was MRS. Henry
Wood.

[1] The Woods then did not build the house but rented
or bought it from city friends.
[2] A wine authority tells me that hock with fish is a
late innovation. How late ?
[3] He would have come either to Guildford (L. & S.W.R.,
L.B. & S.C.R., S.E. & C.R.) or Redhill (S.E. & C.R.,
L.B. & S.C.R.) and changed on to the beautiful bit of
line which runs under Box Hill. Did he also call on
Meredith and Tupper ? It is a key line (in the poem, I
mean, not the railway system) for it helps to date the
verses.
[4] I do not think this refers to the poet's bushy eye-
brows but to the decoration of the hall.
[5] If it is Henry Wood writing, one can well understand
the sad implication.

" Mr. Longfellow, delighted to receive you in our bowers !

Welcome and a thousand welcomes ! Rest you here in
Gomshall Towers ! " [1]

Calmly in his Yankee accent, cultured, carefully and slow

To the greeting of his hostess answered Mr. Longfellow:

" Ma'am, your fine historic mansion[2] is a dream of mine
come true.

'Tis, amid its pines and hemlocks,[3] some Helvetian ren-
dezvous."

In his ivy-mantled bedroom, dirty as he was from town,[4]

'Ere he touched the wash-hand basin[5] did he write a poem
down.

" Little Switzerland in England." What could please a
lady more

Than to find her Surrey mansion had inspired " Excelsior " ?

" Little Switzerland in England," still the name rings in
my ears

When around the bend from Gomshall erstwhile Gomshall
Towers appears.[6]

[1] There is no " Gomshall Towers " on the ordnance
map to-day. Sheet 170 London S.W. 1 inch. Ordnance
Survey Office, Chessington, 1945.
[2] The poet must be in error. There is no *old* mansion
at Gomshall. But he may well have thought Gomshall
Towers old because of the crenellations, and historic
because of its hostess.
[3] Mr. C. E. Cherry, Parks Superintendent of the Lon-
don Borough of Sutton, kindly pointed out (March 1967)
information which calls for my original note to be
amended. He suggests with very sound evidence and

252

wide knowledge that the poet must have been refer-
ring to the hemlock spruces which belong to the *genus
Tsuga*. These are elegant evergreen coniferous trees with
leaves like those of a yew, usually with horizontal
branches and drooping branchlets. He is inclined to
specify the *Tsuga canadensis* because it succeeds in chalk
soil such as to be found in the Gomshall district. This
genus is represented also on both sides of North America.

[4] The word " town " for London was in fashionable
use until this century.

[5] There would not, of course, have been running water
in the bedroom. We are to envisage a brass can with
a face-towel over it. The water may have been cold
and the poet therefore wrote the poem while waiting for
a fresh can to be brought. We must not lightly accuse
him of uncleanliness.

[6] Though the road bends here, I think the railway is
intended, for it is more elevated and commands a view
of the larger houses.

How to Get On in Society

Originally set as a competition in " Time and Tide "

Phone for the fish-knives, Norman
  As Cook is a little unnerved;
You kiddies have crumpled the serviettes
  And I must have things daintily served.

Are the requisites all in the toilet ?
  The frills round the cutlets can wait
Till the girl has replenished the cruets
  And switched on the logs in the grate.

It's ever so close in the lounge, dear,
  But the vestibule's comfy for tea
And Howard is out riding on horseback
  So do come and take some with me.

Now here is a fork for your pastries
  And do use the couch for your feet;
I know what I wanted to ask you—
  Is trifle sufficient for sweet ?

Milk and then just as it comes dear ?

    I'm afraid the preserve's full of stones;

Beg pardon, I'm soiling the doileys

    With afternoon tea-cakes and scones.

Variation on a Theme by
T. W. Rolleston

Under the ground, on a Saturday afternoon in winter
  Lies a mother of five,
And frost has bitten the purple November rose flowers
  Which budded when *she* was alive.

They have switched on the street lamps here by the cemet'ry
                                           railing;
  In the dying afternoon
Men from football, and women from Timothy White's and
                                          McIlroy's
  Will be coming teawards soon.

But her place is empty in the queue at the International,
  The greengrocer's queue lacks one,
So does the crowd at MacFisheries.   There's no one to go
                                          to Freeman's
  To ask if the shoes are done.

Will she, who was so particular, be glad to know that after

The tears, the prayers and the priest,

Her clothing coupons and ration book were handed in at
the Food Office

For the files marked " deceased " ?

Diary of a Church Mouse

(Lines, written to order on a set subject, to be spoken on the wireless.)

Here among long-discarded cassocks,
Damp stools, and half-split open hassocks,
Here where the Vicar never looks
I nibble through old service books.
Lean and alone I spend my days
Behind this Church of England baize.
I share my dark forgotten room
With two oil-lamps and half a broom.
The cleaner never bothers me,
So here I eat my frugal tea.
My bread is sawdust mixed with straw;
My jam is polish for the floor.

Christmas and Easter may be feasts
For congregations and for priests,
And so may Whitsun.   All the same,
They do not fill my meagre frame.
For me the only feast at all

Is Autumn's Harvest Festival,
When I can satisfy my want
With ears of corn around the font.
I climb the eagle's brazen head
To burrow through a loaf of bread.
I scramble up the pulpit stair
And gnaw the marrows hanging there

    It is enjoyable to taste
These items ere they go to waste,
But how annoying when one finds
That other mice with pagan minds
Come into church my food to share
Who have no proper business there.
Two field mice who have no desire
To be baptized, invade the choir.
A large and most unfriendly rat
Comes in to see what we are at.
He says he thinks there is no God
And yet he comes . . . it's rather odd.
This year he stole a sheaf of wheat
(It screened our special preacher's seat),
And prosperous mice from fields away
Come in to hear the organ play,
And under cover of its notes

Ate through the altar's sheaf of oats.
A Low Church mouse, who thinks that I
Am too papistical, and High,
Yet somehow doesn't think it wrong
To munch through Harvest Evensong,
While I, who starve the whole year through,
Must share my food with rodents who
Except at this time of the year
Not once inside the church appear.

Within the human world I know
Such goings-on could not be so,
For human beings only do
What their religion tells them to.
They read the Bible every day
And always, night and morning, pray,
And just like me, the good church mouse,
Worship each week in God's own house,

But all the same it's strange to me
How very full the church can be
With people I don't see at all
Except at Harvest Festival.

Wantage Bells

Now with the bells through the apple bloom
   Sunday-ly sounding
And the prayers of the nuns in their chapel gloom
   Us all surrounding,
  Where the brook flows
  Brick walls of rose
Send on the motionless meadow the bell notes rebounding.

  Wall flowers are bright in their beds
   And their scent all pervading,
  Withered are primroses heads
   And the hyacinth fading
  But flowers by the score
  Multitudes more
Weed flowers and seed flowers and mead flowers our paths
          are invading.

  Where are the words to express
   Such a reckless bestowing ?

The voices of birds utter less
        Than the thanks we are owing,
    Bell notes alone
    Ring praise of their own
As clear as the weed-waving brook and as evenly flowing

Winthrop Mackworth Redivivus

It's for Regency now I'm enthusing
  So we've Regency stripes on the wall
And—my dear, really frightf'lly amusing—
  A dome of wax fruit in the hall.
We've put the Van Gogh in the bathroom,
  Those sunflowers looked *so* out of date,
But instead, as there's plenty of hearth room,
  Real ivy grows out of the grate.

And plants for indoors are the fashion—
  Or so the *News Chronicle* said—
So I've ventured some housekeeping cash on
  A cactus which seems to be dead.
An artist with whom we're acquainted
  Has stippled the dining-room stove
And the walls are alternately painted
  Off-yellow and festival mauve.

The Minister's made the decision
  That Cedric's department must stay

263

So an O.B.E. (Civil Division)

   Will shortly be coming his way.

To you, dear, and also to me, dear,

   It's nothing, for you are a friend,

Not even if you and I see, dear,

   A knighthood, perhaps, in the end.

But it wasn't for this that I fill'd a

   Whole page up with gossip of course.

No: I'm dreadf'lly concerned for Matilda

   Who seems to believe she's a horse.

She neighs when we're sitting at table

   And clutches a make-believe rein.

Her playroom she fancies a stable.

   Do you think she is going insane ?

I know I would not let them christen her—

   Such an old superstition's absurd—

But when Cedric was reading *The Listener*

   Before he tuned in to the Third,

She walked on all fours like a dumb thing

   And nibbled my plants, I'm afraid.

Do you think we could exorcize something

   If we called in the Church to our aid ?

Ex-horse-ize—that's rather funny—
  But it's not very funny to me
For I've spent all her grandmother's money
  On analysis since she was three.
And just when we'd freed her libido
  We went off to Venice and Rome
(You'll remember we met on the Lido)
  And left dear Matilda at home.

I'm afraid that that Riding School did it,
  The one where we sent her to stay;
Were she horse-mad before, then she hid it
  Or her analyst kept it at bay.
But that capable woman in Surrey
  Who seemed so reliable too,
Said " Leave her to me and don't worry,
  This place is as good as the Zoo.

When she's not on a horse she's not idle;
  She can muck out the stables and clean
Her snaffle and saddle and bridle
  Till bed-time at seven-fifteen."
Twenty guineas a week was the price, dear,
  For Matilda it may have been bliss,
But for us it is not very nice, dear,
  To find it has left her like this.

False Security

I remember the dread with which I at a quarter past four
Let go with a bang behind me our house front door
And, clutching a present for my dear little hostess tight,
Sailed out for the children's party into the night
Or rather the gathering night.   For still some boys
In the near municipal acres were making a noise
Shuffling in fallen leaves and shouting and whistling
And running past hedges of hawthorn, spikey and bristling.
And black in the oncoming darkness stood out the trees
And pink shone the ponds in the sunset ready to freeze
And all was still and ominous waiting for dark
And the keeper was ringing his closing bell in the park
And the arc lights started to fizzle and burst into mauve
As I climbed West Hill to the great big house in The Grove,
Where the children's party was and the dear little hostess.
But halfway up stood the empty house where the ghost is
I crossed to the other side and under the arc
Made a rush for the next kind lamp-post out of the dark
And so to the next and the next till I reached the top

Where the Grove branched off to the left.   Then ready to
drop

I ran to the ironwork gateway of number seven

Secure at last on the lamplit fringe of Heaven.

Oh who can say how subtle and safe one feels

Shod in one's children's sandals from Daniel Neal's,

Clad in one's party clothes made of stuff from Heal's ?

And who can still one's thrill at the candle shine

On cakes and ices and jelly and blackcurrant wine,

And the warm little feel of my hostess's hand in mine ?

Can I forget my delight at the conjuring show ?

And wasn't I proud that I was the last to go ?

Too overexcited and pleased with myself to know

That the words I heard my hostess's mother employ

To a guest departing, would ever diminish my joy,

I WONDER WHERE JULIA FOUND THAT STRANGE, RATHER
COMMON LITTLE BOY ?

Eunice

With her latest roses happily encumbered
   Tunbridge Wells Central takes her from the night,
Sweet second bloomings frost has faintly umbered
   And some double dahlias waxy red and white.

Shut again till April stands her little hutment
   Peeping over daisies Michaelmas and mauve,
Lock'd is the Elsan in its brick abutment
   Lock'd the little pantry, dead the little stove.

Keys with Mr. Groombridge, but nobody will take them
   To her lonely cottage by the lonely oak,
Potatoes in the garden but nobody to bake them,
   Fungus in the living room and water in the coke.

I can see her waiting on this chilly Sunday
   For the five forty (twenty minutes late),
One of many hundreds to dread the coming Monday
   To fight with influenza and battle with her weight.

Tweed coat and skirt that with such anticipation
    On a merry spring time a friend had trimm'd with fur,
Now the friend is married and, oh desolation,
    Married to the man who might have married *her*.

High in Onslow Gardens where the soot flakes settle
    An empty flat is waiting her struggle up the stair
And when she puts the wireless on, the heater and the kettle
    It's cream and green and cosy, but home is never there.

Home's here in Kent and how many morning coffees
    And hurried little lunch hours of planning will be spent
Through the busy months of typing in the office
    Until the days are warm enough to take her back to Kent.

Monody on the Death of Aldersgate Street Station

Snow falls in the buffet of Aldersgate station,
  Soot hangs in the tunnel in clouds of steam.
City of London ! before the next desecration
  Let your steepled forest of churches be my theme.

Sunday Silence ! with every street a dead street,
  Alley and courtyard empty and cobbled mews,
Till " tingle tang " the bell of St. Mildred's Bread Street
  Summoned the sermon taster to high box pews,

And neighbouring towers and spirelets joined the ringing
  With answering echoes from heavy commercial walls
Till all were drowned as the sailing clouds went singing
  On the roaring flood of a twelve-voiced peal from Paul's.

Then would the years fall off and Thames run slowly;
  Out into marshy meadow-land flowed the Fleet:
And the walled-in City of London, smelly and holy,
  Had a tinkling mass house in every cavernous street.

The bells rang down and St. Michael Paternoster
    Would take me into its darkness from College Hill,
Or Christ Church Newgate Street (with St. Leonard Foster)
    Would be late for Mattins and ringing insistent still.

Last of the east wall sculpture, a cherub gazes
    On broken arches, rosebay, bracken and dock,
Where once I heard the roll of the Prayer Book phrases
    And the sumptuous tick of the old west gallery clock.

Snow falls in the buffet of Aldersgate station,
    Toiling and doomed from Moorgate Street puffs the train,
For us of the steam and the gas-light, the lost generation,
    The new white cliffs of the City are built in vain.

Thoughts on "The Diary of a Nobody"

The Pooters walked to Watney Lodge
   One Sunday morning hot and still
Where public footpaths used to dodge
   Round elms and oaks to Muswell Hill.

That burning buttercuppy day
   The local dogs were curled in sleep,
The writhing trunks of flowery May
   Were polished by the sides of sheep.

And only footsteps in a lane
   And birdsong broke the silence round
And chuffs of the Great Northern train
   For Alexandra Palace bound.

The Watney Lodge I seem to see
   Is gabled gothic hard and red,
With here a monkey puzzle tree
   And there a round geranium bed.

Each mansion, each new-planted pine,
  Each short and ostentatious drive
Meant Morning Prayer and beef and wine
  And Queen Victoria alive.

Dear Charles and Carrie, I am sure,
  Despite that awkward Sunday dinner,
Your lives were good and more secure
  Than ours at cocktail time in Pinner.

Longfellow's Visit to Venice

(To be read in a quiet New England accent)

Near the celebrated Lido where the breeze is fresh and free
Stands the ancient port of Venice called the City of the Sea.

All its streets are made of water, all its homes are brick
and stone,
Yet it has a picturesqueness which is justly all its own.

Here for centuries have artists come to see the vistas quaint,
Here Bellini set his easel, here he taught his School to paint.

Here the youthful Giorgione gazed upon the domes and
towers,
And interpreted his era in a way which pleases ours.

A later artist, Tintoretto, also did his paintings here,
Massive works which generations have continued to revere.

Still to-day come modern artists to portray the buildings
fair
And their pictures may be purchased on San Marco's famous
Square.

When the bell notes from the belfries and the campaniles
chime

Still to-day we find Venetians elegantly killing time

In their gilded old palazzos, while the music in our ears

Is the distant band at Florians mixed with songs of gon-
doliers.

Thus the New World meets the Old World and the senti-
ments expressed

Are melodiously mingled in my warm New England breast.

Felixstowe, or
The Last of Her Order

With one consuming roar along the shingle
   The long wave claws and rakes the pebbles down
To where its backwash and the next wave mingle,
   A mounting arch of water weedy-brown
Against the tide the off-shore breezes blow.
Oh wind and water, this is Felixstowe.

In winter when the sea winds chill and shriller
   Than those of summer, all their cold unload
Full on the gimcrack attic of the villa
   Where I am lodging off the Orwell Road,
I put my final shilling in the meter
And only make my loneliness completer.

In eighteen ninety-four when we were founded,
   Counting our Reverend Mother we were six,
How full of hope we were and prayer-surrounded
   " The Little Sisters of the Hanging Pyx ".

We built our orphanage. We ran our school.
Now only I am left to keep the rule.

Here in the gardens of the Spa Pavilion
    Warm in the whisper of a summer sea,
The cushioned scabious, a deep vermilion,
    With white pins stuck in it, looks up at me
A sun-lit kingdom touched by butterflies
And so my memory of winter dies.

Across the grass the poplar shades grow longer
    And louder clang the waves along the coast.
The band packs up. The evening breeze is stronger
    And all the world goes home to tea and toast.
I hurry past a cakeshop's tempting scones
Bound for the red brick twilight of St. John's.

" Thou knowest my down sitting and mine uprising "
    Here where the white light burns with steady glow
Safe from the vain world's silly sympathizing,
    Safe with the Love that I was born to know,
Safe from the surging of the lonely sea
My heart finds rest, my heart finds rest in Thee.

Pershore Station,
or *A Liverish Journey First Class*

The train at Pershore station was waiting that Sunday night

Gas light on the platform, in my carriage electric light,

Gas light on frosty evergreens, electric on Empire wood,

The Victorian world and the present in a moment's neigh-
bourhood.

There was no one about but a conscript who was saying
good-bye to his love

On the windy weedy platform with the sprinkled stars above

When sudden the waiting stillness shook with the ancient
spells

Of an older world than all our worlds in the sound of the
Pershore bells.

They were ringing them down for Evensong in the lighted
abbey near,

Sounds which had poured through apple boughs for seven
centuries here.

With Guilt, Remorse, Eternity the void within me fills

And I thought of her left behind me in the Herefordshire
hills.

I remembered her defencelessness as I made my heart a
stone

Till she wove her self-protection round and left me on my
own.

And plunged in a deep self pity I dreamed of another wife

And lusted for freckled faces and lived a separate life.

One word would have made her love me, one word would
have made her turn

But the word I never murmured and now I am left to burn.

Evesham, Oxford and London. The carriage is new and
smart.

I am cushioned and soft and heated with a deadweight in
my heart.

Hertfordshire

I had forgotten Hertfordshire,
   The large unwelcome fields of roots
Where with my knickerbockered sire
   I trudged in syndicated shoots;

And that unlucky day when I
   Fired by mistake into the ground
Under a Lionel Edwards sky
   And felt disapprobation round.

The slow drive home by motor-car,
   A heavy Rover Landaulette,
Through Welwyn, Hatfield, Potters Bar,
   Tweed and cigar smoke, gloom and wet:

" How many times must I explain
   The way a boy should hold a gun ? "
I recollect my father's pain
   At such a milksop for a son.

And now I see these fields once more
    Clothed, thank the Lord, in summer green,
Pale corn waves rippling to a shore
    The shadowy cliffs of elm between,

Colour-washed cottages reed-thatched
    And weather-boarded water mills,
Flint churches, brick and plaster patched,
    On mildly undistinguished hills—

They still are there.   But now the shire
    Suffers a devastating change,
Its gentle landscape strung with wire,
    Old places looking ill and strange.

One can't be sure where London ends,
    New towns have filled the fields of root
Where father and his business friends
    Drove in the Landaulette to shoot;

Tall concrete standards line the lane,
    Brick boxes glitter in the sun:
Far more would these have caused him pain
    Than my mishandling of a gun.

Lord Cozens Hardy

Oh Lord Cozens Hardy
  Your mausoleum is cold,
The dry brown grass is brittle
  And frozen hard the mould
And where those Grecian columns rise
  So white among the dark
Of yew trees and of hollies in
  That corner of the park
By Norfolk oaks surrounded
  Whose branches seem to talk,
I know, Lord Cozens Hardy,
  I would not like to walk.

And even in the summer,
  On a bright East-Anglian day
When round your Doric portico
  Your children's children play
There's a something in the stillness
  And our waiting eyes are drawn

From the butler and the footman
   Bringing tea out on the lawn,
From the little silver spirit lamp
   That burns so blue and still,
To the half-seen mausoleum
   In the oak trees on the hill.

But when, Lord Cozens Hardy,
   November stars are bright,
And the King's Head Inn at Letheringsett
   Is shutting for the night,
The villagers have told me
   That they do not like to pass
Near your curious mausoleum
   Moon-shadowed on the grass
For fear of seeing walking
   In the season of All Souls
That first Lord Cozens Hardy,
   The Master of the Rolls.

Variation on a Theme by Newbolt

The City will see him no more at important meetings
   In Renaissance board rooms by Edwin Cooper designed;
In his numerous clubs the politely jocular greetings
   Will be rather more solemn to-day with his death in mind.

Half mast from a first floor window, the Company's bunting
   Flops over Leadenhall Street in this wintry air
And his fellow directors, baulked of a good day's hunting
   Nod gloomily back to the gloomy commissionaire.

His death will be felt through the whole of the organization,
   In every branch of its vast managerial tree,
His brother-in-law we suppose will attend the cremation,
   A service will later be held in St. Katherine Cree.

But what of his guns ?—he was always a generous giver.
   (Oh yes, of course, we will each of us send a wreath),
His yacht ? and his shoot ? and his beautiful reach of
                      river ?
   And all the clubs in his locker at Walton Heath ?

284

I do not know, for my mind sees one thing only,
    A luxurious bedroom looking on miles of fir
From a Surrey height where his widow sits silent and lonely
    For the man whose love seemed wholly given to her.

Inevitable

First there was putting hot-water bottles to it,
    Then there was seeing what an osteopath could do,
Then trying drugs to coax the thing and woo it,
    Then came the time when he knew that he was through.

Now in his hospital bed I see him lying
    Limp on the pillows like a cast-off Teddy bear.
Is he too ill to know that he is dying ?
    And, if he does know, does he really care ?

Grey looks the ward with November's overcasting
    But his large eyes seem to see beyond the day;
Speech becomes sacred near silence everlasting
    Oh if I *must* speak, have I words to say ?

In the past weeks we had talked about Variety,
    Vesta Victoria, Lew Lake and Wilkie Bard,
Horse-buses, hansoms, crimes in High Society—
    Although we knew his death was near, we fought against
                                                    it hard.

Now from his remoteness in a stillness unaccountable

    He drags himself to earth again to say good-bye to me—

His final generosity when almost insurmountable

    The barriers and mountains he has crossed again must be.

N.W.5 & N.6

Red cliffs arise.   And up them service lifts
Soar with the groceries to silver heights.
Lissenden Mansions.   And my memory sifts
Lilies from lily-like electric lights
And Irish stew smells from the smell of prams
And roar of seas from roar of London trams.

Out of it all my memory carves the quiet
Of that dark privet hedge where pleasures breed,
There first, intent upon its leafy diet,
I watched the looping caterpillar feed
And saw it hanging in a gummy froth
Till, weeks on, from the chrysalis burst the moth.

I see black oak twigs outlined on the sky,
Red squirrels on the Burdett-Coutts estate.
I ask my nurse the question " Will I die ? "
As bells from sad St. Anne's ring out so late,
" And if I do die, will I go to Heaven ? "
Highgate at eventide.   Nineteen-eleven.

" You will.   I won't."   From that cheap nursery-maid,
Sadist and puritan as now I see,
I first learned what it was to be afraid,
Forcibly fed when sprawled across her knee
Lock'd into cupboards, left alone all day,
" World without end."   What fearsome words to pray.

" World without end."   It was not what she'ld do
That frightened me so much as did her fear
And guilt at endlessness.   I caught them too,
Hating to think of sphere succeeding sphere
Into eternity and God's dread will.
I caught her terror then.   I have it still.

From the Great Western

These small West Country towns where year by year
Newly elected mayors oppose reforms
Their last year's Worships promised—down the roads
Large detached houses, Croydons of the West,
Blister in summer heat; striped awnings hang
Over front doors, and those geraniums,
Retired tradesmen love to cultivate,
Blaze in the gravel.   From more furtive streets
Unmarried mothers leave for London.   Girls
Who had such promise suddenly lose their looks.
Small businesses go bankrupt.   Corners once
Familiar for a shuttered toll gate house
Are smoothed away to make amenities.
The copper beech, the bunchy sycamore
And churchyard limes are felled.   Among their stumps
The almond tree shall flourish.   Corn Exchange—
On with the Poultry Show ! and Cemet'ry,
With your twin chapels, safely gather in
Church and dissent from small West Country towns
Where year by year,
Newly elected Mayors oppose reforms.

In the Public Gardens

In the Public Gardens,
 To the airs of Strauss,
Eingang we're in love again
 When *ausgang* we were *aus*.

The waltz was played, the songs were sung,
 The night resolved our fears;
From bunchy boughs the lime trees hung
 Their gold electroliers.

Among the loud Americans
 Zwei Engländer were we,
You so white and frail and pale
 And me so deeply me;

I bought for you a dark-red rose,
 I saw your grey-green eyes,
As high above the floodlights,
 The true moon sailed the skies.

In the Public Gardens,
        Ended things begin;
    Ausgang we were out of love
        Und eingang we are in.

Preface to " High and Low "

MURRAY, you bid my plastic pen
A preface write.   Well, here's one then.
Verse seems to me the shortest way
Of saying what one has to say,
A memorable means of dealing
With mood or person, place or feeling.
Anything extra that is given
Is taken as a gift from Heaven.

    The English language has such range,
Such rhymes and half-rhymes, rhythms strange,
And such variety of tone,
It is a music of its own.
With MILTON it has organ power
As loud as bells in Redcliffe tower;
It falls like winter crisp and light
On COWPER's Buckinghamshire night.
It can be gentle as a lake,
Where WORDSWORTH's oars a ripple make
Or rest with TENNYSON at ease

In sibilance of summer seas,
Or languorous as lilies grow,
When DOWSON's lamp is burning low—
For endless changes can be rung
On church-bells of the English tongue.

   MURRAY, your venerable door
Opened to BYRON, CRABBE and MOORE
And TOMMY CAMPBELL.   How can I,
A buzzing insubstantial fly,
Compare with them ?   I do not try,
Pleased simply to be one who shares
An imprint that was also theirs,
And grateful to the people who
Have bought my verses hitherto.

Cornish Cliffs

Those moments, tasted once and never done,
Of long surf breaking in the mid-day sun.
A far-off blow-hole booming like a gun—

The seagulls plane and circle out of sight
Below this thirsty, thrift-encrusted height,
The veined sea-campion buds burst into white

And gorse turns tawny orange, seen beside
Pale drifts of primroses cascading wide
To where the slate falls sheer into the tide.

More than in gardened Surrey, nature spills
A wealth of heather, kidney-vetch and squills
Over these long-defended Cornish hills.

A gun-emplacement of the latest war
Looks older than the hill fort built before
Saxon or Norman headed for the shore.

And in the shadowless, unclouded glare
Deep blue above us fades to whiteness where
A misty sea-line meets the wash of air.

Nut-smell of gorse and honey-smell of ling
Waft out to sea the freshness of the spring
On sunny shallows, green and whispering.

The wideness which the lark-song gives the sky
Shrinks at the clang of sea-birds sailing by
Whose notes are tuned to days when seas are high.

From today's calm, the lane's enclosing green
Leads inland to a usual Cornish scene—
Slate cottages with sycamore between,

Small fields and tellymasts and wires and poles
With, as the everlasting ocean rolls,
Two chapels built for half a hundred souls

Tregardock

A mist that from the moor arose
    In sea-fog wraps Port Isaac bay,
The moan of warning from Trevose
    Makes grimmer this October day.

Only the shore and cliffs are clear.
    Gigantic slithering sholves of slate
In waiting awfulness appear
    Like journalism full of hate.

On the steep path a bramble leaf
    Stands motionless and wet with dew,
The grass bends down, the bracken's brown,
    The grey-green gorse alone is new.

Cautious my sliding footsteps go
    To quarried rock and dripping cave;
The ocean, leaden-still below,
    Hardly has strength to lift a wave.

I watch it crisp into its height
    And flap exhausted on the beach,
The long surf menacing and white
    Hissing as far as it can reach.

The dunlin do not move, each bird
    Is stationary on the sand
As if a spirit in it heard
    The final end of sea and land.

And I on my volcano edge
    Exposed to ridicule and hate
Still do not dare to leap the ledge
    And smash to pieces on the slate.

By the Ninth Green, St Enodoc

Dark of primaeval pine encircles me
With distant thunder of an angry sea
While wrack and resin scent alternately
    The air I breathe.

On slate compounded before man was made
The ocean ramparts roll their light and shade
Up to Bray Hill and, leaping to invade,
    Fall back and seethe.

A million years of unrelenting tide
Have smoothed the strata of the steep cliffside:
How long ago did rock with rock collide
    To shape these hills?

One day the mayfly's life, three weeks the cleg's,
The woodworm's four-year cycle bursts its eggs,
The flattened centipede lets loose its legs
    And stings and kills.

Hot life pulsating in this foreshore dry,
Damp life upshooting from the reed-beds high,
Under those barrows, dark against the sky,
    The Iron Age dead—

Why is it that a sunlit second sticks?
What force collects all this and seeks to fix
This fourth March morning nineteen sixty-six
    Deep in my head?

Winter Seascape

The sea runs back against itself
  With scarcely time for breaking wave
To cannonade a slatey shelf
  And thunder under in a cave

Before the next can fully burst.
  The headwind, blowing harder still,
Smooths it to what it was at first—
  A slowly rolling water-hill.

Against the breeze the breakers haste,
  Against the tide their ridges run
And all the sea's a dappled waste
  Criss-crossing underneath the sun.

Far down the beach the ripples drag
  Blown backward, rearing from the shore,
And wailing gull and shrieking shag
  Alone can pierce the ocean roar.

Unheard, a mongrel hound gives tongue,
   Unheard are shouts of little boys:
What chance has any inland lung
   Against this multi-water noise?

Here where the cliffs alone prevail
   I stand exultant, neutral, free,
And from the cushion of the gale
   Behold a huge consoling sea.

Old Friends

The sky widens to Cornwall.   A sense of sea
  Hangs in the lichenous branches and still there's light.
The road from its tunnel of blackthorn rises free
        To a final height,

And over the west is glowing a mackerel sky
  Whose opal fleece has faded to purple pink.
In this hour of the late-lit, listening evening, why
        Do my spirits sink?

The tide is high and a sleepy Atlantic sends
  Exploring ripple on ripple down Polzeath shore,
And the gathering dark is full of the thought of friends
        I shall see no more.

Where is Anne Channel who loved this place the best,
  With her tense blue eyes and her shopping-bag falling
                                              apart,
And her racy gossip and nineteen-twenty zest,
        And that warmth of heart?

303

Where's Roland, easing his most unwieldy car,
  With its load of golf-clubs, backwards into the lane?
Where Kathleen Stokes with her Sealyhams? There's Doom Bar;
      Bray Hill shows plain;

For this is the turn, and the well-known trees draw near;
  On the road their pattern in moonlight fades and swells:
As the engine stops, from two miles off I hear
      St Minver bells.

What a host of stars in a wideness still and deep:
  What a host of souls, as a motor-bike whines away
And the silver snake of the estuary curls to sleep
      In Daymer Bay.

Are they one with the Celtic saints and the years between?
  Can they see the moonlit pools where ribbonweed drifts?
As I reach our hill, I am part of a sea unseen—
      The oppression lifts.

A Bay in Anglesey

The sleepy sound of a tea-time tide
Slaps at the rocks the sun has dried,

Too lazy, almost, to sink and lift
Round low peninsulas pink with thrift.

The water, enlarging shells and sand,
Grows greener emerald out from land

And brown over shadowy shelves below
The waving forests of seaweed show.

Here at my feet in the short cliff grass
Are shells, dried bladderwrack, broken glass,

Pale blue squills and yellow rock roses.
The next low ridge that we climb discloses

One more field for the sheep to graze
While, scarcely seen on this hottest of days,

Far to the eastward, over there,
Snowdon rises in pearl-grey air.

Multiple lark-song, whispering bents,
The thymy, turfy and salty scents

And filling in, brimming in, sparkling and free
The sweet susurration of incoming sea.

A Lament for Moira McCavendish

Through the midlands of Ireland I journeyed by diesel
    And bright in the sun shone the emerald plain;
Though loud sang the birds on the thorn-bush and teasel
    They could not be heard for the sound of the train.

The roll of the railway made musing creative:
    I thought of the colleen I soon was to see
With her wiry black hair and grey eyes of the native,
    Sweet Moira McCavendish, acushla machree.

Her brother's wee cabin stands distant from Tallow
    A league and a half, where the Blackwater flows,
And the musk and potato, the mint and the mallow
    Do grow there in beauty, along with the rose.

'Twas smoothly we raced through the open expansion
    Of rush-covered levels and gate-lodge and gate
And the ruined demesne and the windowless mansion
    Where once the oppressor had revelled in state.

At Castletownroche, as the prospect grew hillier,
  I saw the far mountains to Moira long-known
Till I came to the valley and townland familiar
  With the Protestant church standing locked and alone.

O vein of my heart! upon Tallow Road Station
  No face was to greet me, so freckled and white;
As the diesel slid out, leaving still desolation,
  The McCavendish ass-cart was nowhere in sight.

For a league and half to the Blackwater river
  I tramped with my bundle her cabin to see
And herself by the fuchsias, her young lips a-quiver
  Half-smiling, half-weeping a welcome to me.

Och Moira McCavendish! the fangs of the creeper
  Have struck at the thatch and thrust open the door;
The couch in the garden grows ranker and deeper
  Than musk and potato which bloomed there before.

Flow on, you remorseless and salmon-full waters!
  What care I for prospects so silvery fair?
The heart in me's dead, like your sweetest of daughters,
  And I would that my spirit were lost on the air.

The Small Towns of Ireland

Public houses in Irish country towns are very often general merchants as well. You drink at a counter with bacon on it. Brooms and plastic dustpans hang from the ceiling. Loaves of new bread are stacked on top of fuse wire and, over all, there is a deep, delicious silence that can be found only in Ireland, in the midlands of Ireland in particular—the least touristed and profoundest part of that whole sad, beautiful country. Much that is native and traditional goes on, including the printing of ballads in metres derived from the Celts via Tom Moore. These ballads are called hedge poetry and their authors are the last descendants of the Gaelic bards. It was in just such a general shop as I have described that I might have found, pinned up among the notices for a local Feis, Gaelic football matches and Government proclamations, the following ballad, printed on emerald paper in a border of shamrocks.

The small towns of Ireland by bards are neglected,

They stand there, all lonesome, on hilltop and plain.

The Protestant glebe house by beech trees protected

Sits close to the gates of his Lordship's demesne.

But where is his Lordship, who once in a phaeton

Drove out twixt his lodges and into the town?

Oh his tragic misfortunes I will not dilate on;
   His mansion's a ruin, his woods are cut down.

His impoverished descendant is dwelling in Ealing,
   His daughters must type for their bread and their board,
O'er the graves of his forebears the nettle is stealing
   And few will remember the sad Irish Lord.

Yet still stands the Mall where his agent resided,
   The doctor, attorney and such class of men.
The elegant fanlights and windows provided
   A Dublin-like look for the town's Upper Ten.

'Twas bravely they stood by the Protestant steeple
   As over the town rose their roof-trees afar.
Let us slowly descend to the part where the people
   Do mingle their ass-carts by Finnegan's bar.

I hear it once more, the soft sound of those voices,
   When fair day is filling with farmers the Square,
And the heart in my bosom delights and rejoices
   To think of the dealing and drinking done there.

I see thy grey granite, O grim House of Sessions!
   I think of the judges who sat there in state

And my mind travels back to our monster processions
    To honour the heroes of brave Ninety-Eight.

The barracks are burned where the Redcoats oppressed us,
    The gaol is broke open, our people are free.
Though Cromwell once cursed us, Saint Patrick has blessed
                                       us—
    The merciless English have fled o'er the sea.

Look out where yon cabins grow smaller to smallest,
    Straw-thatched and one-storey and soon to come down,
To the prominent steeple, the newest and tallest,
    Of Saint Malachy's Catholic Church in our town:

The fine architécture, the wealth of mosaic,
    The various marbles on altars within—
To attempt a description were merely prosaic,
    So, asking your pardon, I will not begin.

O my small town of Ireland, the raindrops caress you,
    The sun sparkles bright on your field and your Square
As here on your bridge I salute you and bless you,
    Your murmuring waters and turf-scented air.

Ireland's Own
or
The Burial of Thomas Moore

In the churchyard of Bromham the yews intertwine
O'er a smooth granite cross of a Celtic design,
Looking quite out of place in surroundings like these
In a corner of Wilts 'twixt the chalk and the cheese.

I can but account you neglected and poor,
Dear bard of my boyhood, mellifluous Moore,
That far from the land which of all you loved best
In a village of England your bones should have rest.

I had rather they lay where the Blackwater glides
When the light of the evening doth burnish its tides
And St Carthage Cathedral's meticulous spire
Is tipped like the Castle with sun-setting fire.

I had rather some gate-lodge of plaster and thatch
With slim pointed windows and porches to match

Had last seen your coffin drawn out on the road
From a great Irish house to its final abode.

Or maybe a rath with a round tower near
And the whispering Shannon delighting the ear
And the bog all around and the width of the sky
Is the place where your bones should deservedly lie.

The critics may scorn you and Hazlitt may carp
At the ' Musical Snuff-box ' you made of the Harp;
The Regency drawing-rooms that thrilled with your song
Are not the true world to which now you belong.

No! the lough and the mountain, the ruins and rain
And purple-blue distances bound your demesne,
For the tunes to the elegant measures you trod
Have chords of deep longing for Ireland and God.

Great Central Railway
Sheffield Victoria to Banbury

' Unmitigated England '
   Came swinging down the line
That day the February sun
   Did crisp and crystal shine.
Dark red at Kirkby Bentinck stood
   A steeply gabled farm
' Mid ash trees and a sycamore
   In charismatic calm.
A village street—a manor house—
   A church—then, tally ho!
We pounded through a housing scheme
   With tellymasts a-row,
Where cars of parked executives
   Did regimented wait
Beside administrative blocks
   Within the factory gate.
She waved to us from Hucknall South
   As we hooted round a bend,

From a curtained front-room window did
   The diesel driver's friend.
Through cuttings deep to Nottingham
   Precariously we wound;
The swallowing tunnel made the train
   Seem London's Underground.
Above the fields of Leicestershire
   On arches we were borne
And the rumble of the railway drowned
   The thunder of the Quorn;
And silver shone the steeples out
   Above the barren boughs;
Colts in a paddock ran from us
   But not the solid cows;
And quite where Rugby Central is
   Does only Rugby know.
We watched the empty platform wait
   And sadly saw it go.
By now the sun of afternoon
   Showed ridge and furrow shadows
And shallow unfamiliar lakes
   Stood shivering in the meadows.
Is Woodford church or Hinton church
   The one I ought to see?

Or were they both too much restored
    In 1883?
I do not know.   Towards the west
    A trail of glory runs
And we leave the old Great Central line
    For Banbury and buns.

Matlock Bath

From Matlock Bath's half-timbered station
   I see the black dissenting spire—
Thin witness of a congregation,
   Stone emblem of a Handel choir;
In blest Bethesda's limpid pool
Comes treacling out of Sunday School.

By cool Siloam's shady rill—
   The sounds are sweet as strawberry jam:
I raise mine eyes unto the hill,
   The beetling HEIGHTS OF ABRAHAM;
The branchy trees are white with rime
In Matlock Bath this winter-time,

And from the whiteness, grey uprearing,
   Huge cliffs hang sunless ere they fall,
A tossed and stony ocean nearing
   The moment to o'erwhelm us all:

317

Eternal Father, strong to save,
How long wilt thou suspend the wave?

How long before the pleasant acres
    Of intersecting LOVERS' WALKS
Are rolled across by limestone breakers,
    Whole woodlands snapp'd like cabbage stalks?
O God, our help in ages past,
How long will SPEEDWELL CAVERN last?

In this dark dale I hear the thunder
    Of houses folding with the shocks,
The GRAND PAVILION buckling under
    The weight of the ROMANTIC ROCKS,
The hardest Blue John ash-trays seem
To melt away in thermal steam.

Deep in their Nonconformist setting
    The shivering children wait their doom—
The father's whip, the mother's petting
    In many a coffee-coloured room;
And attic bedrooms shriek with fright,
For dread of *Pilgrims of the Night.*

Perhaps it's this that makes me shiver
  As I ascend the slippery path
High, high above the sliding river
  And terraces of Matlock Bath:
A sense of doom, a dread to see
The *Rock of Ages cleft for me.*

An Edwardian Sunday
Broomhill, Sheffield

High dormers are rising
So sharp and surprising,
And ponticum edges
The driveways of gravel;
Stone houses from ledges
Look down on ravines.
The vision can travel
From gable to gable,
Italianate mansion
And turretted stable,
A sylvan expansion
So varied and jolly
Where laurel and holly
Commingle their greens.

Serene on a Sunday
The sun glitters hotly
O'er mills that on Monday

With engines will hum.
By tramway excursion
To Dore and to Totley
In search of diversion
The millworkers come;
But in our arboreta
The sounds are discreeter
Of shoes upon stone —
The worshippers wending
To welcoming chapel,
Companioned or lone;
And over a pew there
See loveliness lean,
As Eve shows her apple
Through rich bombazine:
What love is born new there
In blushing eighteen!

Your prospects will please her,
The iron-king's daughter,
Up here on Broomhill:
Strange Hallamshire, County
Of dearth and of bounty,
Of brown tumbling water
And furnace and mill.

Your own Ebenezer*

Looks down from his height

On back street and alley

And chemical valley

Laid out in the light;

On ugly and pretty

Where industry thrives

In this hill-shadowed city

Of razors and knives.

* The statue of Ebenezer Elliott (1781–1849) the 'Corn
Law Rhymer' outside the Mappin Gallery, Sheffield.

Lines written to Martyn Skinner before his Departure from Oxfordshire in Search of Quiet—1961

Return, return to Ealing,
    Worn poet of the farm!
Regain your boyhood feeling
    Of uninvaded calm!
For there the leafy avenues
    Of lime and chestnut mix'd
Do widely wind, by art designed,
    The costly houses 'twixt.

No early morning tractors
    The thrush and blackbird drown,
No nuclear reactors
    Bulge huge below the down,
No youth upon his motor-bike
    His lust for power fulfils,
With dentist's drill intent to kill
    The silence of the hills.

323

In Ealing on a Sunday
  Bell-haunted quiet falls,
In Ealing on a Monday
  'Milk-o!' the milkman calls;
No lorries grind in bottom gear
  Up steep and narrow lanes,
Nor constant here offend the ear
  Low-flying aeroplanes.

Return, return to Ealing,
  Worn poet of the farm!
Regain your boyhood feeling
  Of uninvaded calm!
Where smoothly glides the bicycle
  And softly flows the Brent
And a gentle gale from Perivale
  Sends up the hayfield scent.

Uffington

Tonight we feel the muffled peal
  Hang on the village like a pall;
It overwhelms the towering elms—
  That death-reminding dying fall;
The very sky no longer high
  Comes down within the reach of all.
Imprisoned in a cage of sound
Even the trivial seems profound.

Anglo-Catholic Congresses

We, who remember the Faith, the grey-headed ones,
  Of those Anglo-Catholic Congresses swinging along,
Who heard the South Coast salvo of incense-guns
  And surged to the Albert Hall in our thousands strong
  With 'extreme' colonial bishops leading in song;

We, who remember, look back to the blossoming May-time
  On ghosts of servers and thurifers after Mass,
The slapping of backs, the flapping of cassocks, the play-
                                                    time,
  A game of Grandmother's Steps on the vicarage grass—
  "Father, a little more sherry.   I'll fill your glass."

We recall the triumph, that Sunday after Ascension,
  When our Protestant suffragan suffered himself to be
                                                    coped—
The SYA and the Scheme for Church Extension —
  The new diocesan's not as 'sound' as we'd hoped,
  And Kensit threatens and has Sam Gurney poped?

326

Yet, under the Travers baroque, in a limewashed whiteness,
  The fiddle-back vestments a-glitter with morning rays,
Our Lady's image, in multiple-candled brightness,
  The bells and banners—those were the waking days
  When Faith was taught and fanned to a golden blaze.

In Willesden Churchyard

Come walk with me, my love, to Neasden Lane.
The chemicals from various factories
Have bitten deep into the Portland stone
And streaked the white Carrara of the graves
Of many a Pooter and his Caroline,
Long laid to rest among these dripping trees;
And that small heap of fast-decaying flowers
Marks Lupin Pooter lately gathered in;
And this, my love, is Laura Seymour's grave—
' So long the loyal counsellor and friend '
Of that Charles Reade whose coffin lies with hers.
Was she his mistress?   Did he visit her
When coming down from Oxford by the coach?
Alighting at the turnpike, did he walk
These elmy lanes of Middlesex and climb
A stile or two across the dairy farms
Over to Harlesden at the wicket gate?
Then the soft rigours of his Fellowship
Were tenderly relaxed.   The sun would send

Last golden streaks of mild October light
On tarred and weather-boarded barn and shed.
Blue bonfire smoke would hang among the trees;
And in the little stucco hermitage
Did Laura gently stroke her lover's head?
And did her Charles look up into her eyes
For loyal counsel there?   I do not know.
Doubtless some pedant for his Ph.D.
Has ascertained the facts, or I myself
Might find them in the public libraries.
I only know that as we see her grave
My flesh, to dissolution nearer now
Than yours, which is so milky white and soft,
Frightens me, though the Blessed Sacrament
Not ten yards off in Willesden parish church
Glows with the present immanence of God.

The Commander

On a shining day of October we remembered you,
Commander,
   When the trees were gold and still
And some of their boughs were green where the whip of the
wind had missed them
   On this nippy Staffordshire hill.

A clean sky streamed through institutional windows
   As we heard the whirr of Time
Touching our Quaker silence, in builders' lorries departing
   For Newcastle-under-Lyme.

The proving words of the psalm you bequeathed to the
gowned assembly
   On waiting silence broke,
' Lord, I am not high-minded . . .'   In the youthful voice
of the student
   Your own humility spoke.

I remembered our shared delight in architecture and nature
   As bicycling we went

330

By saffron-spotted palings to crumbling box-pewed churches
    Down hazel lanes in Kent.

I remembered on winter evenings, with wine and the family
                       round you,
    Your reading Dickens aloud
And the laughs we used to have at your gift for administra-
                       tion,
    For you were never proud.

Sky and sun and the sea! the greatness of things was in you
    And thus you refrained your soul.
Let others fuss over academical detail,
    You saw people whole.

' Lord, I am not high-minded . . .'   The final lesson you
                       taught me,
    When you bade the world good-bye,
Was humbly and calmly to trust in the soul's survival
    When my own hour comes to die.

Autumn 1964

(FOR KAREN)

Red apples hang like globes of light
　　Against this pale November haze,
And now, although the mist is white,
　　In half-an-hour a day of days
Will climb into its golden height
　　And Sunday bells will ring its praise.

The sparkling flint, the darkling yew,
　　The red brick, less intensely red
Than hawthorn berries bright with dew
　　Or leaves of creeper still unshed,
The watery sky washed clean and new,
　　Are all rejoicing with the dead.

The yellowing elm shows yet some green,
　　The mellowing bells exultant sound:
Never have light and colour been
　　So prodigally thrown around;
And in the bells the promise tells
　　Of greater light where Love is found.

The Hon. Sec.

The flag that hung half-mast to-day
  Seemed animate with being
As if it knew for whom it flew
  And will no more be seeing.

He loved each corner of the links—
  The stream at the eleventh,
The grey-green bents, the pale sea-pinks,
  The prospect from the seventh;

To the ninth tee the uphill climb,
  A grass and sandy stairway,
And at the top the scent of thyme
  And long extent of fairway.

He knew how on a summer day
  The sea's deep blue grew deeper,
How evening shadows over Bray
  Made that round hill look steeper.

He knew the ocean mists that rose
  And seemed for ever staying,
When moaned the foghorn from Trevose
  And nobody was playing;

The flip of cards on winter eves,
  The whisky and the scoring,
As trees outside were stripped of leaves
  And heavy seas were roaring.

He died when early April light
  Showed red his garden sally
And under pale green spears glowed white
  His lilies of the valley:

That garden where he used to stand
  And where the robin waited
To fly and perch upon his hand
  And feed till it was sated.

The Times would never have the space
  For Ned's discreet achievements;
The public prints are not the place
  For intimate bereavements.

A gentle guest, a willing host,
    Affection deeply planted—
It's strange that those we miss the most
    Are those we take for granted.

Monody on the Death of a Platonist Bank Clerk

This is the lamp where he first read Whitman
    Out of the library large and free.
Every quarter the bus to Kirkstall
    Stopped and waited, but on read he.

This was his room with books in plenty:
    Dusty, now I have raised the blind—
Fenimore Cooper, Ballantyne, Henty,
    Edward Carpenter wedged behind.

These are the walls adorned with portraits,
    Camera studies and Kodak snaps;
'Camp at Pevensey'—'Scouts at Cleethorpes'—
    There he is with the lads and chaps.

This is the friend, the best and greatest,
    Pure in his surplice, smiling, true—

336

The enlarged Photomaton—that's the latest,
   Next to the coloured one ' August Blue '.

These are his pipes.   Ah! how he loved them,
   Puffed and petted them, after walks,
After tea and a frowst with crumpets,
   Puffed the smoke into serious talks.

All the lot of them, how they came to him—
   Tea and chinwag—gay young lives!
Somehow they were never the same to him
   When they married and brought their wives.

Good-bye

Some days before death
 When food's tasting sour on my tongue,
Cigarettes long abandoned,
 Disgusting now even champagne;
When I'm sweating a lot
 From the strain on a last bit of lung
And lust has gone out
 Leaving only the things of the brain;
More worthless than ever
 Will seem all the songs I have sung,
More harmless the prods of the prigs,
 Remoter the pain,
More futile the Lord Civil Servant
 As, rung upon rung,
He ascends by committees to roofs
 Far below on the plain.
But better down there in the battle
 Than here on the hill
With Judgement or nothingness waiting me.
 Lonely and chill.

Five o'Clock Shadow

This is the time of day when we in the Men's Ward
  Think "One more surge of the pain and I give up the
                                          fight,"
When he who struggles for breath can struggle less strongly:
  This is the time of day which is worse than night.

A haze of thunder hangs on the hospital rose-beds,
  A doctors' foursome out on the links is played,
Safe in her sitting-room Sister is putting her feet up:
  This is the time of day when we feel betrayed.

Below the windows, loads of loving relations
  Rev in the car park, changing gear at the bend,
Making for home and a nice big tea and the telly:
  " Well, we've done what we can.   It can't be long till the
                                          end."

This is the time of day when the weight of bedclothes
  Is harder to bear than a sharp incision of steel.
The endless anonymous croak of a cheap transistor
  Intensifies the lonely terror I feel.

A Russell Flint

I could not speak for amazement at your beauty
    As you came down the Garrick stair,
Grey-green eyes like the turbulent Atlantic
    And floppy schoolgirl hair.

I could see you in a Sussex teashop,
    Dressed in peasant weave and brogues,
Turning over, as firelight shone on brassware,
    Last year's tea-stained *Vogues*.

I could see you as a large-eyed student,
    Frowning as you tried to learn,
Or, head flung back, the confident girl prefect,
    Thrillingly kind and stern.

I could not speak for amazement at your beauty;
    Yet, when you spoke to me,
You were calm and gentle as a rock pool
    Waiting, warm, for the sea.

Wave on wave, I plunged in them to meet you—
　In wave on wave I drown;
Calm rock pool, on the shore of my security
　Hold me when the tide goes down.

Perp. Revival i' the North

O, I wad gang tae Harrogate
    Tae a kirk by Temple Moore,
Wi' a tall choir and a lang nave
    And rush mats on the floor;
And Percy Dearmer chasubles
    And nae pews but chairs,
And there we'll sing the Sarum rite
    Tae English Hymnal airs.

It's a far cry frae Harrogate
    And mony a heathery mile
Tae a stane kirk wi' a wee spire
    And a verra wee south aisle.
The rhododendrons bloom wi'oot
    On ilka Simmer's day,
And it's there the Airl o' Feversham
    Wad hae his tenants pray;
For there's something in the painted roof
    And the mouldings round the door,
The braw bench and the plain font
    That tells o' Temple Moore.

Agricultural Caress

Keep me from Thelma's sister Pearl!
She puts my senses in a whirl,
Weakens my knees and keeps me waiting
Until my heart stops palpitating.

The debs may turn disdainful backs
On Pearl's uncouth mechanic slacks,
And outraged see the fire that lies
And smoulders in her long-lashed eyes.

Have they such weather-freckled features,
The smooth sophisticated creatures?
Ah, not to them such limbs belong,
Such animal movements sure and strong,

Such arms to take a man and press
In agricultural caress
His head to hers, and hold him there
Deep buried in her chestnut hair.

343

God shrive me from this morning lust
For supple farm girls: if you must,
Send the cold daughter of an earl—
But spare me Thelma's sister Pearl!

Narcissus

Yes, it was Bedford Park the vision came from—
   de Morgan lustre glowing round the hearth,
And that sweet flower which self-love takes its name from
   Nodding among the lilies in the garth,
And Arnold Dolmetsch touching the spinet,
And Mother, Chiswick's earliest suffragette.

I was a delicate boy—my parents' only—
   And highly strung.   My father was in trade.
And how I loved, when Mother left me lonely,
   To watch old Martha spice the marmalade,
Or help with flower arrangements in the lobby
Before I went to find my playmate Bobby.

We'ld go for walks, we bosom boyfriends would
   (For Bobby's watching sisters drove us mad),
And when we just did nothing we were good,
   But when we touched each other we were bad.
I found this out when Mother said one day
She thought we were unwholesome in our play.

345

So Bobby and I were parted.   Bobby dear,
   I didn't want my tea.   I heard your sisters
Playing at hide-and-seek with you quite near
   As off the garden gate I picked the blisters.
Oh tell me, Mother, what I mustn't do—
Then, Bobby, I can play again with you.

For I know hide-and-seek's most secret places
   More than your sisters do.   And you and I
Can scramble into them and leave no traces,
   Nothing above us but the twigs and sky,
Nothing below us but the leaf-mould chilly
Where we can warm and hug each other silly.

My Mother wouldn't tell me why she hated
   The things we did, and why they pained her so.
She said a fate far worse than death awaited
   People who did the things we didn't know,
And then she said I was her precious child,
And once there was a man called Oscar Wilde.

" Open your story book and find a tale
   Of ladyes fayre and deeds of derring-do,
Or good Sir Gawaine and the Holy Grail,

Mother will read her boy a page or two
Before she goes, this Women's Suffrage Week,
To hear that clever Mrs Pankhurst speak.

Sleep with your hands above your head. That's right—
    And let no evil thoughts pollute the dark.''
She rose, and lowered the incandescent light.
    I heard her footsteps die down Bedford Park.
Mother where are you?   Bobby, Bobby, where?
I clung for safety to my teddy bear.

The Cockney Amorist

Oh when my love, my darling,
    You've left me here alone,
I'll walk the streets of London
    Which once seemed all our own.

The vast suburban churches
    Together we have found:
The ones which smelt of gaslight
    The ones in incense drown'd;
I'll use them now for praying in
    And not for looking round.

No more the Hackney Empire
    Shall find us in its stalls
When on the limelit crooner
    The thankful curtain falls,
And soft electric lamplight
    Reveals the gilded walls.

I will not go to Finsbury Park
    The putting course to see
Nor cross the crowded High Road
    To Williamsons' to tea,
For these and all the other things
    Were part of you and me.

I love you, oh my darling,
    And what I can't make out
Is why since you have left me
    I'm somehow still about.

Harvest Hymn

We spray the fields and scatter
   The poison on the ground
So that no wicked wild flowers
   Upon our farm be found.
We like whatever helps us
   To line our purse with pence;
The twenty-four-hour broiler-house
   And neat electric fence.

All concrete sheds around us
   And Jaguars in the yard,
The telly lounge and deep-freeze
   Are ours from working hard.

We fire the fields for harvest,
   The hedges swell the flame,
The oak trees and the cottages
   From which our fathers came.
We give no compensation,

The earth is ours today,
And if we lose on arable,
Then bungalows will pay.

All concrete sheds . . . etc.

Meditation on the A30

A man on his own in a car
   Is revenging himself on his wife;
He opens the throttle and bubbles with dottle
   And puffs at his pitiful life.

" She's losing her looks very fast,
   She loses her temper all day;
That lorry won't let me get past,
   This Mini is blocking my way.

" Why can't you step on it and shift her!
   I can't go on crawling like this!
At breakfast she said that she wished I was dead—
   Thank heavens we don't have to kiss.

" I'd like a nice blonde on my knee
   And one who won't argue or nag.
Who dares to come hooting at *me*?
   I only give way to a Jag.

" You're barmy or plastered, I'll pass you, you bastard—
  I *will* overtake you.   I *will*! "
As he clenches his pipe, his moment is ripe
  And the corner's accepting its kill.

Inexpensive Progress

Encase your legs in nylons,
Bestride your hills with pylons
 O age without a soul;
Away with gentle willows
And all the elmy billows
 That through your valleys roll.

Let's say good-bye to hedges
And roads with grassy edges
 And winding country lanes;
Let all things travel faster
Where motor-car is master
 Till only Speed remains.

Destroy the ancient inn-signs
But strew the roads with tin signs
 'Keep Left,' 'M4,' 'Keep Out!'
Command, instruction, warning,
Repetitive adorning
 The rockeried roundabout;

For every raw obscenity
Must have its small ' amenity,'
   Its patch of shaven green,
And hoardings look a wonder
In banks of floribunda
   With floodlights in between.

Leave no old village standing
Which could provide a landing
   For aeroplanes to roar,
But spare such cheap defacements
As huts with shattered casements
   Unlived-in since the war.

Let no provincial High Street
Which might be your or my street
   Look as it used to do,
But let the chain stores place here
Their miles of black glass facia
   And traffic thunder through.

And if there is some scenery,
Some unpretentious greenery,
   Surviving anywhere,

It does not need protecting
For soon we'll be erecting
   A Power Station there.

When all our roads are lighted
By concrete monsters sited
   Like gallows overhead,
Bathed in the yellow vomit
Each monster belches from it,
   We'll know that we are dead

Mortality

The first-class brains of a senior civil servant
   Shiver and shatter and fall
As the steering column of his comfortable Humber
   Batters in the bony wall.
All those delicate little re-adjustments
   '' On the one hand, if we proceed
With the *ad hoc* policy hitherto adapted
   To individual need . . .
On the other hand, too rigid an arrangement
   Might, of itself, perforce . . .
I would like to submit for the Minister's concurrence
   The following alternative course,
Subject to revision and reconsideration
   In the light our experience gains . . .''
And this had to happen at the corner where the by-pass
   Comes into Egham out of Staines.
That very near miss for an All Souls' Fellowship
   The recent compensation of a 'K'—
The first-class brains of a senior civil servant
   Are sweetbread on the road today.

357

Reproof Deserved
or
After the Lecture

When I saw the grapefruit drying, cherry in each centre
lying,

And a dozen guests expected at the table's polished oak,

Then I knew, my lecture finished, I'ld be feeling quite
diminished

Talking on, but unprotected, so that all my spirit broke.

"Have you read the last Charles Morgan?" "Are you
writing for the organ

Which is published as a vital adjunct to our cultural
groups?"

"This year some of us are learning all *The Lady's Not for
Burning*

For a poetry recital we are giving to the troops."

"Mr Betjeman, I grovel before critics of the novel,

Tell me, if I don't offend you, have you written one your-
self?

You haven't? Then the one I wrote is (not that I expect a
notice)

Something I would like to send you, just for keeping on
your shelf."

358

" Betjeman, I bet your racket brings you in a pretty packet

  Raising the old lecture curtain, writing titbits here and there.

But, by Jove, your hair is thinner, since you came to us in Pinner,

  And you're fatter now, I'm certain. What you need is country air."

This and that way conversation, till I turn in desperation

  To a kind face (can I doubt it?) mercifully mute so far.

" Oh," it says, " I missed the lecture, wasn't it on architecture?

  Do please tell me all about it, what you do and who you are."

Caprice

I sat only two tables off from the one I was sacked at,
    Just three years ago,
And here was another meringue like the one which I hacked
    at
    When pride was brought low
And the coffee arrived—the place which she had to use tact
    at
    For striking the blow.

" I'm making some changes next week in the organisation
    And though I admire
Your work for me, John, yet the need to increase circulation
    Means you must retire:
An outlook more global than yours is the qualification
    I really require."

Oh sickness of sudden betrayal!   Oh purblind Creator!
    Oh friendship denied!
I stood on the pavement and wondered which loss was the
               greater—

The cash or the pride.
Explanations to make to subordinates, bills to pay later
Churned up my inside.

Cricket Master
(AN INCIDENT)

My undergraduate eyes beholding,
    As I climbed your slope, Cat Hill:
Emerald chestnut fans unfolding,
    Symbols of my hope, Cat Hill,
What cared I for past disaster,
Applicant for cricket master,
Nothing much of cricket knowing,
Conscious but of money owing?
    Somehow I would cope, Cat Hill.

" The sort of man we want must be prepared
To take our first eleven.   Many boys
From last year's team are with us.   You will find
Their bowling's pretty good and they are keen."
" And so am I, Sir, very keen indeed."
Oh where's mid-on?   And what is silly point?
Do six balls make an over?   Help me, God!
" Of course you'll get some first-class cricket too;

The MCC send down an A team here."
My bluff had worked. I sought the common-room,
Of last term's pipe-smoke faintly redolent.
It waited empty with its worn arm-chairs
For senior bums to mine, when in there came
A fierce old eagle in whose piercing eye
I saw that instant-registered dislike
Of all unhealthy aesthetes such as me.
" I'm Winters—you're our other new recruit
And here's another new man—Barnstaple."
He introduced a thick Devonian.
" Let's go and have some practice in the nets.
You'd better go in first." With but one pad,
No gloves, and knees that knocked in utter fright,
Vainly I tried to fend the hail of balls
Hurled at my head by brutal Barnstaple
And at my shins by Winters. Nasty quiet
Followed my poor performance. When the sun
Had sunk behind the fringe of Hadley Wood
And Barnstaple and I were left alone
Among the ash-trays of the common-room,
He murmured in his soft West-country tones:
" D'you know what Winters told me, Betjeman?
He didn't think you'd ever held a bat."

The trusting boys returned.   " We're jolly glad
You're on our side, Sir, in the trial match."
" But I'm no good at all." " Oh yes, you are."
When I was out first ball, they said " Bad luck!
You hadn't got your eye in."   Still I see
Barnstaple's smile of undisguised contempt,
Still feel the sting of Winters' silent sneer.
Disgraced, demoted to the seventh game,
Even the boys had lost their faith in me.
God guards his aesthetes.   If by chance these lines
Are read by one who in some common-room
Has had his bluff called, let him now take heart:
In every school there is a sacred place
More holy than the chapel.   Ours was yours:
I mean, of course, the first-eleven pitch.
Here in the welcome break from morning work,
The heavier boys, of milk and biscuits full,
Sat on the roller while we others pushed
Its weighty cargo slowly up and down.
We searched the grass for weeds, caressed the turf,
Lay on our stomachs squinting down its length
To see that all was absolutely smooth.
    The prize-day neared.   And, on the eve before,
We masters hung our college blazers out

In readiness for tomorrow.   Matron made
A final survey of the boys' best clothes—
Clean shirts.   Clean collars. " Rice, your jacket's torn.
Bring it to me this instant!''   Supper done,
Barnstaple drove his round-nosed Morris out
And he and I and Vera Spencer-Clarke,
Our strong gymnasium mistress, squashed ourselves
Into the front and rattled to The Cock.

Sweet bean-fields then were scenting Middlesex;
Narrow lanes led between the dairy-farms
To ponds reflecting weather-boarded inns.
There on the wooden bench outside The Cock
Sat Barnstaple, Miss Spencer-Clarke and I,
At last forgetful of tomorrow's dread
And gazing into sky-blue Hertfordshire.
Three pints for Barnstaple, three halves for me,
Sherry of course for Vera Spencer-Clarke.

Pre-prize-day nerves ?   Or too much bitter beer ?
What had that evening done to Barnstaple ?
I only know that singing we returned ;
The more we sang, the faster Barnstaple
Drove his old Morris, swerving down the drive
And in and out the rhododendron clumps,
Over the very playing-field itself,

And then—oh horror!—right across the pitch
Not once, but twice or thrice. The mark of tyres
Next day was noticed at the Parents' Match.
That settled Barnstaple and he was sacked,
While I survived him, lasting three more terms.

Shops and villas have invaded
    Your chestnut quiet there, Cat Hill.
Cricket field and pitch degraded,
    Nothing did they spare, Cat Hill.
Vera Spencer-Clarke is married
And the rest are dead and buried;
I am thirty summers older,
Richer, wickeder and colder,
    Fuller too of care, Cat Hill.